LANDMARK DECISIONS OF THE UNITED STATES SUPREME COURT II

MAUREEN HARRISON & STEVE GILBERT
EDITORS

LANDMARK DECISIONS SERIES

EXCELLENT BOOKS
BEVERLY HILLS, CALIFORNIA

EXCELLENT BOOKS
Post Office Box 7121
Beverly Hills, CA 90212-7121

Publisher's Cataloging in Publication Data

Landmark Decisions Of The United States Supreme Court II/
 Maureen Harrison, Steve Gilbert, editors.
 p. cm. - (Landmark Decisions Series)
Bibliography: p.
Includes Index.
1. United States. Supreme Court.
I. Title. II. Harrison, Maureen. III. Gilbert, Steve.
IV. Series: Landmark Decisions.
KF8742.H24 1991   LC 90-84578
347.'73'26-dc20
[347.30726]
ISBN 0-9628014-2-9
ISBN 0-9628014-0-2 (Landmark Decisions Series)

A Note To The Reader

On the first Monday of each October the United States Supreme Court begins a new Term. The Crier of the Court announces, "All persons having business before the Honorable, the Supreme Court of the United States, are admonished to draw near and give their attention, for the Court is now sitting. God save the United States and this Honorable Court." From all over the country, on all kinds of issues, and for all kinds of reasons, Americans bring controversies to the Court for a final disposition. The Founding Fathers created the Supreme Court to construct and interpret the meaning of the Constitution. Chief Justice Charles Evans Hughes summed up the Court's responsibility in this way: "We are under a Constitution, but the Constitution is what the Judges say it is."

The U.S. Supreme Court has the final word on all Constitutional questions arising in the Federal Courts and all Federal questions arising in the State Courts. Since 1791 the Supreme Court has issued thousands of individual decisions. All have been important to the parties involved, but some, a significant few, have grown so important as to involve all Americans. These are Landmark Decisions, fundamentally altering the relationships of Americans to their institutions and to each other. Of these significant few, we have selected ten for inclusion in this book. These decisions, issued over the span of 134 years, represent some of the great controversies of American history and politics. They are presented here in synopsis for the first time to the general reader.

Every year five thousand petitions for review are received by the Court. Four of the nine Justices must agree to a review. Four hundred petitions are accepted. Less than two hundred will result in written decisions. Once accepted, written arguments [briefs] are submitted to the Court and oral arguments are heard. Soon after, the nine Justices meet in conference to vote on whether they will affirm [let stand] or reverse [change the outcome of], in whole or in part, the decisions of the lower courts from which these appeals have come. One Justice, voting in the majority, will be selected to write the majority opinion. Others may join in the majority opinion, write their own concurring opinion, write their own dissenting opinion, or join in another's concurrence or dissent. Drafts of the majority, concurring, and dissenting opinions circulate among the Justices, are redrafted, and recirculated, until a consensus is reached and a decision announced. In some instances the Court will issue its decision *per curiam* [by the court], speaking with one voice without attribution of authorship. It is the majority opinion as finally issued by the Court that stands as the law of the land.

Judge Learned Hand wrote: "The language of the law must not be foreign to the ears of those who are to obey it." The ten Landmark Decisions presented in this book are carefully edited versions of the official texts issued by the Supreme Court in *United States Reports.* The editors have made every effort to replace legalese with reading ease without damaging the original decisions. Edited out are long legal citations and wordy wrangles over points of procedure. Edited in are definitions (*writ of habeas corpus* = an order from a judge to bring a person to court), translations (*certiorari* = the decision of the Court to review a case), identifications (Appellant = Dred Scott, Appellee = John Sandford), and explanations (where the case originated, how it got to the court, and who the parties were). You will find in this book the majority opinion of the Court as expressed by the Justice chosen to speak for the Court. Concurring and dissenting opinions, with a few notable exceptions, have not been included.

Preceding each edited decision, we note where the complete decision can be found. The bibliography provides a list of further reading on the cases and the Court. Also included for the reader's reference is a complete copy of the U.S. Constitution, to which every decision refers.

This is the second book in the **Landmark Decisions Series**. The first dealt with Landmark Decisions on School Desegregation, Obscenity, School Prayer, Fair Trials, Sexual Privacy, Censorship, Abortion, Affirmative Action, Book Banning and Flag Burning. We have tried to give an equal mix of history and politics in this second work and have presented cases on Slavery, Women's Suffrage, the treatment of Japanese Americans in World War II, Bible Reading in Public Schools, Banned Books, Rights of the Accused, the Death Penalty, Homosexuality, Offensive Speech, and the Right To Die. Also included are two non-Supreme Court cases, added for their historical significance.

Chief Justice John Marshall said the Court's decision "comes home in its effects to every man's fireside; it passes on his property, his reputation, his life, his all." We entered into editing this series because we, like you, and your family and friends, must obey, under penalty of law, the decisions of the U.S. Supreme Court. It stands to reason that, if we owe them our obedience, then we owe it to ourselves to know what they say, not second-hand, but for ourselves. We think it's time for you to have the final word.

M.H. & S.G.

This book is dedicated to our mothers,

Florence and Faye

ABOUT THE EDITORS

MAUREEN HARRISON is a textbook editor and a
member of the Supreme Court Historical Society

STEVE GILBERT is a law librarian and a member of the
American Association of Law Libraries and the American
Bar Association

TABLE OF CONTENTS

SLAVERY
13

"[T]hat unfortunate race . . . had for more than a century before been regarded as beings of an inferior order, and altogether unfit to associate with the white race . . . so far inferior, that they had no rights which the white man was bound to respect."
Chief Justice Roger Taney
Dred Scott v. Sandford (1857)

WOMEN'S SUFFRAGE
35

"The right of suffrage, when granted, will be protected. He who has it can only be deprived of it by due process of law, but in order to claim protection he must first show that he has the right."
Chief Justice Morrison Waite
Minor v. Happersett (1875)

"If she believed she had a right to vote, and voted in reliance upon that belief does that relieve her from the penalty? . . . [I]gnorance of the law excuses no one. . . [S]he takes the risk, and she can not escape the consequences. . . ."
Circuit Justice Ward Hunt
United States v. Anthony (1873)

JAPANESE AMERICAN
CONCENTRATION CAMPS
49

" . . . It is said that we are dealing here with the case of imprisonment of a citizen in a concentration camp solely because of his ancestry, without evidence or inquiry concerning his loyalty . . . "
Justice Hugo Black
Korematsu v. United States (1944)

" . . . [I]f any fundamental assumption underlies our system, it is that guilt is personal and not inheritable."
Justice Robert Jackson, dissenting
Korematsu v. United States (1944)

BIBLE READING IN THE PUBLIC SCHOOLS
67

"In the relationship between man and religion, the State is firmly committed to a position of neutrality."
Justice Thomas Clark
Abington School District v. Shempp (1963)

THE BOOK BANNED IN BOSTON
83

"A book cannot be proscribed unless it is found to be *utterly* without redeeming social value."
Justice William Brennan
"Fanny Hill" v. Massachusetts (1966)

RIGHTS OF THE ACCUSED
95

"If the Government becomes a lawbreaker, it breeds contempt for law; it invites every man to become a law unto himself; it invites anarchy."
Chief Justice Earl Warren
Miranda v. Arizona (1966)

THE DEATH PENALTY
115

"'It is the poor, the sick, the ignorant, the powerless and the hated who are executed.'"
Justice William O. Douglas, concurring
Furman v. Georgia (1972)

"'Punishments are cruel when they involve torture or a lingering death; but the punishment of death is not cruel, within the meaning of the word as used in the Constitution.'"
Justice Lewis Powell, dissenting
Furman v. Georgia (1972)

HOMOSEXUALITY
133

"The law, however, is constantly based on notions of morality, and if all laws representing essentially moral choices are to be invalidated under the Due Process Clause, the courts will be very busy indeed."
Justice Byron White
Bowers v. Hardwick (1986)

". . . [T]he homosexual and the hetrosexual have the same interest in deciding how he will live his own life . . ."
Justice John Paul Stevens, dissenting
Bowers v. Hardwick (1986)

OFFENSIVE SPEECH
145

"'[T]he freedom to speak one's mind is not only an aspect of individual liberty - and thus a good unto itself - but also is essential to the common quest for truth and the vitality of society as a whole.'"
Chief Justice William Rehnquist
Hustler v. Falwell (1988)

THE RIGHT TO DIE
157

"The choice between life and death is a deeply personal decision of obvious and overwhelming finality."
Chief Justice William Rehnquist
Cruzan v. Missouri (1990)

"Ultimately there comes a point at which the individual's rights overcome the State interest."
NJ Supreme Court Chief Justice Richard J. Hughes
In The Matter of Karen Ann Quinlan (1976)

THE U.S. CONSTITUTION
193

"We the people of the United States, in order to form a more perfect union, establish justice, insure domestic tranquility, provide for the common defense, promote the general welfare, and secure the blessings of liberty to ourselves and our posterity, do ordain and establish this Constitution for the United States of America."
The Preamble (1789)

BIBLIOGRAPHY *225*

INDEX *231*

SLAVERY

DRED SCOTT v. SANDFORD

Dred Scott, a negro, was born into slavery on a Virginia plantation in 1795. In 1832 he was sold by the plantation owners to U.S. Army doctor John Emerson, then stationed in the slave-holding state of Missouri. In 1834 Dr. Emerson was transferred and removed Scott from the slave-holding state of Missouri to the free state of Illinois. In 1836, with the consent of their owner, Dred Scott married a woman named Harriet, another of Dr. Emerson's slaves whom he had purchased the year before. The Scotts had two children, Eliza and Lizzie. In 1836 Emerson was transferred again, and moved Dred and Harriet Scott, this time to the free territory of Wisconsin. In 1838 Emerson returned with the Scotts to settle in slave-holding Missouri. Dr. Emerson died in 1843. Dred Scott and his family became the property of Emerson's widow, who sold them to her brother, John F.A. Sanford.

Dred Scott sued Sanford (spelled Sandford incorrectly in Court records) for his freedom based on his residence between 1834 and 1838 in a free state and free territory, both created under the Missouri Compromise, which forbade slavery.

In 1854 Scott sued for his freedom in State Court. A St. Louis County jury found for Scott. The Missouri Supreme Court reversed their decision and found for Sandford. Scott then sued for his freedom in Federal Court. Sandford countered that Scott, a Negro, did not have the right to sue. An appeal was taken to the U.S. Supreme Court. The case was argued twice, first in February and again in December 1856.

On March 6, 1857 Chief Justice Roger B. Taney delivered the decision of the Court.

The complete text of *Dred Scott v. Sandford* appears in volume 60 of *United States Reports.*

DRED SCOTT v. SANDFORD

March 6, 1857

CHIEF JUSTICE ROGER TANEY: The plaintiff [Dred Scott] . . . was, with his wife [Harriet] and children [Eliza and Lizzie], held as slaves by the defendant [John F.A. Sandford], in the State of Missouri; and [Scott] brought this action in the [United States Circuit Court] for that district, to assert the [right] of himself and his family to freedom.

. . . . [Sandford] pleaded . . . that [Scott] was not a citizen of the State of Missouri . . . being a negro of African descent, whose ancestors were of pure African blood, and who were brought into this country and sold as slaves.

. . . . The question is simply this: Can a negro, whose ancestors were imported into this country, and sold as slaves, become a member of the political community formed and brought into existence by the Constitution of the United States, and as such become entitled to all the rights, and privileges, and immunities, guarantied by that instrument to the citizen? One of which rights is the privilege of suing in a court of the United States in the cases specified in the Constitution.

. . . . The words "people of the United States" and "citizens" are synonymous. . . . They both describe the political body who, according to our republican institutions, form the sovereignty, and who hold the power and conduct the Government through their representatives. They are what we familiarly call the "sovereign people," and every citizen is one of this people,

and a constituent member of this sovereignty. The
question before us is, whether the class of persons
described in the plea . . . compose a portion of this people,
and are constituent members of this sovereignty? We
think they are not, and that they are not included, and
were not intended to be included, under the word
"citizens" in the Constitution, and can therefore claim
none of the rights and privileges which that instrument
provides for and secures to citizens of the United States.
On the contrary, they were at that time considered as a
subordinate and inferior class of beings, who had been
subjugated by the dominant race, and, whether
emancipated or not, yet remained subject to their
authority, and had no rights or privileges but such as
those who held the power and the Government might
choose to grant them.

It is not the province of the court to decide upon the
justice or injustice, the policy or impolicy, of these laws.
The decision of that question belonged to the political or
law-making power; to those who formed the sovereignty
and framed the Constitution. The duty of the court is, to
interpret the instrument they have framed, with the best
lights we can obtain on the subject, and to administer it as
we find it, according to its true intent and meaning when
it was adopted.

. . . . It is very clear . . . that no State can, by any act or
law of its own, passed since the adoption of the
Constitution, introduce a new member into the political
community created by the Constitution of the United
States. It cannot make him a member of this community
by making him a member of its own. And for the same
reason it cannot introduce any person, or description of
persons, who were not intended to be embraced in this

new political family, which the Constitution brought into existence, but were intended to be excluded from it.

The question then arises, whether the provisions of the Constitution, in relation to the personal rights and privileges to which the citizen of a State should be entitled, embraced the negro African race, at that time in this country, or who might afterwards be imported, who had then or should afterwards be made free in any State; and to put it in the power of a single State to make him a citizen of the United States, and endue him with the full rights of citizenship in every other State without their consent? Does the Constitution of the United States act upon him whenever he shall be made free under the laws of a State, and raised there to the rank of a citizen, and immediately clothe him with all the privileges of a citizen in every other State, and in its own courts?

The court think the affirmative of these propositions cannot be maintained. And if it cannot, [Scott] could not be a citizen of the State of Missouri, within the meaning of the Constitution of the United States, and, consequently, was not entitled to sue in its courts.

It is true, every person, and every class and description of persons, who were at the time of the adoption of the Constitution recognised as citizens in the several States, became also citizens of this new political body; but none other; it was formed by them, and for them and their posterity, but for no one else. And the personal rights and privileges guarantied to citizens of this new sovereignty were intended to embrace those only who were then members of the several State communities, or who should afterwards by birthright or otherwise become members, according to the provisions of the Constitution and the principles on which it was founded. It was the union of those who were at that time members of distinct and separate political communities into one political family, whose power, for certain specified purposes, was to extend over the whole territory of the United States. And it gave to each citizen rights and privileges outside of his State which he did not before possess, and placed him in every other State upon a perfect equality with its own citizens as to rights of person and rights of property; it made him a citizen of the United States.

It becomes necessary, therefore, to determine who were citizens of the several States when the Constitution was adopted. And in order to do this, we must recur [go back] to the Governments and institutions of the thirteen colonies, when they separated from Great Britain and formed new sovereignties, and took their places in the family of independent nations. We must inquire who, at that time, were recognised as the people or citizens of a State, whose rights and liberties had been outraged by the English Government; and who declared their independence, and assumed the powers of Government to defend their rights by force of arms.

In the opinion of the court, the legislation and histories of the times, and the language used in the Declaration of Independence, show, that neither the class of persons who had been imported as slaves, nor their descendants, whether they had become free or not, were then acknowledged as a part of the people, nor intended to be included in the general words used in that memorable instrument.

It is difficult at this day to realize the state of public opinion in relation to that unfortunate race, which prevailed in the civilized and enlightened portions of the world at the time of the Declaration of Independence, and when the Constitution of the United States was framed and adopted. But the public history of every European nation displays it in a manner too plain to be mistaken.

They had for more than a century before been regarded as beings of an inferior order, and altogether unfit to associate with the white race, either in social or political relations; and so far inferior, that they had no rights which the white man was bound to respect; and that the negro might justly and lawfully be reduced to slavery for his benefit. He was bought and sold, and treated as an ordinary article of merchandise and traffic, whenever a profit could be made by it. This opinion was at that time fixed and universal in the civilized portion of the white race. It was regarded as an axiom in morals as well as in politics, which no one thought of disputing, or supposed to be open to dispute; and men in every grade and position in society daily and habitually acted upon it in their private pursuits, as well as in matters of public concern, without doubting for a moment the correctness of this opinion.

And in no nation was this opinion more firmly fixed or more uniformly acted upon than by the English Government and English people. They not only seized them on the coast of Africa, and sold them or held them in slavery for their own use; but they took them as ordinary articles of merchandise to every country where they could make a profit on them, and were far more extensively engaged in this commerce than any other nation in the world.

The opinion thus entertained and acted upon in England was naturally impressed upon the colonies they founded on this side of the Atlantic. And, accordingly, a negro of the African race was regarded by them as an article of property, and held, and bought and sold as such, in every one of the thirteen colonies which united in the Declaration of Independence, and afterwards formed the Constitution of the United States. The slaves were more or less numerous in the different colonies, as slave labor was found more or less profitable. But no one seems to have doubted the correctness of the prevailing opinion of the time.

. . . . The language of the Declaration of Independence is equally conclusive:

It begins by declaring that, "when in the course of human events it becomes necessary for one people to dissolve the political bands which have connected them with another, and to assume among the powers of the earth the separate and equal station to which the laws of nature and nature's God entitle them, a decent respect for the opinions of mankind requires that they should declare the causes which impel them to the separation."

It then proceeds to say: "We hold these truths to be self-evident: that all men are created equal; that they are endowed by their Creator with certain unalienable rights; that among them is life, liberty, and the pursuit of happiness; that to secure these rights, Governments are instituted, deriving their just powers from the consent of the governed."

The general words above quoted would seem to embrace the whole human family, and if they were used in a similar instrument at this day would be so understood. But it is too clear for dispute, that the enslaved African race were not intended to be included, and formed no part of the people who framed and adopted this declaration; for if the language, as understood in that day, would embrace them, the conduct of the distinguished men who framed the Declaration of Independence would have been utterly and flagrantly inconsistent with the principles they asserted; and instead of the sympathy of mankind, to which they so confidently appealed, they would have deserved and received universal rebuke and reprobation.

Yet the men who framed this declaration were great men - high in literary acquirements - high in their sense of honor, and incapable of asserting principles inconsistent with those on which they were acting. They perfectly understood the meaning of the language they used, and how it would be understood by others; and they knew that it would not in any part of the civilized world be supposed to embrace the negro race, which, by common consent, had been excluded from civilized Governments and the family of nations, and doomed to slavery. They spoke and acted according to the then established doctrines and principles, and in the ordinary language of the day, and no one misunderstood them. The unhappy black race were separated from the white by indelible marks, and laws long before established, and were never thought of or spoken of except as property, and when the claims of the owner or the profit of the trader were supposed to need protection.

This state of public opinion had undergone no change when the Constitution was adopted, as is equally evident from its provisions and language.

The brief preamble sets forth by whom it was formed, for what purposes, and for whose benefit and protection. It declares that it is formed by the *people* of the United States; that is to say, by those who were members of the different political communities in the several States; and its great object is declared to be to secure the blessings of liberty to themselves and their posterity. It speaks in general terms of the *people* of the United States, and of *citizens* of the several States, when it is providing for the exercise of the powers granted or the privileges secured to the citizen. It does not define what description of persons are intended to be included under these terms, or who shall be regarded as a citizen and one of the people. It uses them as terms so well understood, that no further description or definition was necessary.

But there are two clauses in the Constitution which point directly and specifically to the negro race as a separate class of persons, and show clearly that they were not regarded as a portion of the people or citizens of the Government then formed.

One of these clauses reserves to each of the thirteen States the right to import slaves until the year 1808, if it thinks proper. And the importation which it thus sanctions was unquestionably of persons of the race of which we are speaking, as the traffic in slaves in the United States had always been confined to them. And by the other provision the States pledge themselves to each other to maintain the right of property of the master, by delivering up to him any slave who may have escaped from his service, and be found within their respective territories. By the first above-mentioned clause, therefore, the right to purchase and hold this property is directly sanctioned and authorized for twenty years by the people who framed the Constitution. And by the second, they pledge themselves to maintain and uphold the right of the master in the manner specified, as long as the Government they then formed should endure. And these two provisions show, conclusively, that neither the description of persons therein referred to, nor their descendants, were embraced in any of the other provisions of the Constitution; for certainly these two clauses were not intended to confer on them or their posterity the blessings of liberty, or any of the personal rights so carefully provided for the citizen.

No one of that race had ever migrated to the United States voluntarily; all of them had been brought here as articles of merchandise. The number that had been emancipated at that time were but few in comparison with those held in slavery; and they were identified in the public mind with the race to which they belonged, and regarded as a part of the slave population rather than the free. It is obvious that they were not even in the minds of the framers of the Constitution when they were conferring special rights and privileges upon the citizens of a State in every other part of the Union.

Indeed, when we look to the condition of this race in the several States at the time, it is impossible to believe that these rights and privileges were intended to be extended to them.

It is very true, that in the portion of the Union where the labor of the negro race was found to be unsuited to the climate and unprofitable to the master, but few slaves were held at the time of the Declaration of Independence; and when the Constitution was adopted, it had entirely worn out in one of them, and measures had been taken for

its gradual abolition in several others. But this change
had not been produced by any change of opinion in
relation to this race; but because it was discovered, from
experience, that slave labor was unsuited to the climate
and productions of these States: for some of the States,
where it had ceased or nearly ceased to exist, were
actively engaged in the slave trade, procuring cargoes on
the coast of Africa, and transporting them for sale to
those parts of the Union where their labor was found to
be profitable, and suited to the climate and productions.
And this traffic was openly carried on, and fortunes
accumulated by it, without reproach from the people of
the States where they resided. And it can hardly be
supposed that, in the States where it was then
countenanced in its worst form - that is, in the seizure and
transportation - the people could have regarded those who
were emancipated as entitled to equal rights with
themselves.

. . . . The legislation of [several] States [Maryland,
Connecticut, New Hampshire, Rhode Island,
Massachusetts] . . . shows, in a manner not to be mistaken,
the inferior and subject condition of that race at the time
the Constitution was adopted, and long afterwards,
throughout the thirteen States by which that instrument
was framed; and it is hardly consistent with the respect
due to these States, to suppose that they regarded at that
time, as fellow-citizens and members of the sovereignty, a
class of beings whom they had thus stigmatized; whom, as
we are bound, out of respect to the State sovereignties, to
assume they had deemed it just and necessary thus to
stigmatize, and upon whom they had impressed such deep
and enduring marks of inferiority and degradation; or,
that when they met in convention to form the
Constitution, they looked upon them as a portion of their

constituents, or designed to include them in the provisions so carefully inserted for the security and protection of the liberties and rights of their citizens. It cannot be supposed that they intended to secure to them rights, and privileges, and rank, in the new political body throughout the Union, which every one of them denied within the limits of its own dominion. More especially, it cannot be believed that the large slaveholding States regarded them as included in the word citizens, or would have consented to a Constitution which might compel them to receive them in that character from another State. For if they were so received, and entitled to the privileges and immunities of citizens, it would exempt them from the operation of the special laws and from the police regulations which they considered to be necessary for their own safety. It would give to persons of the negro race, who were recognised as citizens in any one State of the Union, the right to enter every other State whenever they pleased, singly or in companies, without pass or passport, and without obstruction, to sojourn there as long as they pleased, to go where they pleased at every hour of the day or night without molestation, unless they committed some violation of law for which a white man would be punished; and it would give them the full liberty of speech in public and in private upon all subjects upon which its own citizens might speak; to hold public meetings upon political affairs, and to keep and carry arms wherever they went. And all of this would be done in the face of the subject race of the same color, both free and slaves, and inevitably producing discontent and insubordination among them, and endangering the peace and safety of the State.

It is impossible, it would seem, to believe that the great men of the slaveholding States, who took so large a share

in framing the Constitution of the United States, and
exercised so much influence in procuring its adoption,
could have been so forgetful or regardless of their own
safety and the safety of those who trusted and confided in
them.

. . . . A clause similar to the one in the Constitution, in
relation to the rights and immunities of citizens of one
State in the other States, was contained in the Articles of
Confederation.   But there is a difference of language,
which is worthy of note. The provision in the Articles of
Confederation was, "that the *free inhabitants* of each of
the States, paupers, vagabonds, and fugitives from justice,
excepted, should be entitled to all the privileges and
immunities of free citizens in the several States."

It will be observed, that under this Confederation, each
State had the right to decide for itself, and in its own
tribunals, whom it would acknowledge as a free inhabitant
of another State.   The term *free inhabitant*, in the
generality of its terms, would certainly include one of the
African race who had been [freed from slavery]. But no
example, we think, can be found of his admission to all
the privileges of citizenship in any State of the Union
after these Articles were formed, and while they
continued in force. And, notwithstanding the generality
of the words "free inhabitants," it is very clear that,
according to their accepted meaning in that day, they did
not include the African race, whether free or not: for the
fifth section of the ninth article provides that Congress
should have the power "to agree upon the number of land
forces to be raised, and to make requisitions from each
State for its quota in proportion to the number of *white*
inhabitants in such State, which requisition should be
binding."

Words could hardly have been used which more strongly mark the line of distinction between the citizen and the subject; the free and the subjugated races. The latter were not even counted when the inhabitants of a State were to be embodied in proportion to its numbers for the general defence. And it cannot for a moment be supposed, that a class of persons thus separated and rejected from those who formed the sovereignty of the States, were yet intended to be included under the words "free inhabitants," in the preceding article, to whom privileges and immunities were so carefully secured in every State.

But although this clause of the Articles of Confederation is the same in principle with that inserted in the Constitution, yet the comprehensive word *inhabitant*, which might be construed to include an emancipated slave, is omitted; and the privilege is confined to *citizens* of the State. And this alteration in words would hardly have been made, unless a different meaning was intended to be conveyed, or a possible doubt removed. The just and fair inference is, that as this privilege was about to be placed under the protection of the General Government, and the words expounded by its tribunals, and all power in relation to it taken from the State and its courts, it was deemed prudent to describe with precision and caution the persons to whom this high privilege was given - and the word *citizen* was on that account substituted for the words *free inhabitant*. The word citizen excluded, and no doubt intended to exclude, foreigners who had not become citizens of some one of the States when the Constitution was adopted; and also every description of persons who were not fully recognised as citizens in the several States. This, upon any fair construction of the instruments to which we have referred, was evidently the object and purpose of this change of words.

To all this mass of proof we have still to add, that Congress has repeatedly legislated upon the same construction of the Constitution that we have given. Three laws, two of which were passed almost immediately after the Government went into operation, will be abundantly sufficient to show this. The two first are particularly worthy of notice, because many of the men who assisted in framing the Constitution, and took an active part in procuring its adoption, were then in the halls of legislation, and certainly understood what they meant when they used the words "people of the United States" and "citizen" in that well-considered instrument.

The first of these acts is the naturalization law, which was passed at the second session of the first Congress, March 26, 1790, and confines the right of becoming citizens "*to aliens being free white persons.*"

Now, the Constitution does not limit the power of Congress in this respect to white persons. And they may, if they think proper, authorize the naturalization of any one, of any color, who was born under allegiance to another Government. But the language of the law above quoted, shows that citizenship at that time was perfectly understood to be confined to the white race; and that they alone constituted the sovereignty in the Government.

. . . . Another of the early laws of which we have spoken, is the first militia law, which was passed in 1792, at the first session of the second Congress. The language of this law is equally plain and significant with the one just mentioned. It directs that every "free able-bodied white male citizen" shall be enrolled in the militia. The word *white* is evidently used to exclude the African race, and the word "citizen" to exclude unnaturalized foreigners; the latter forming no part of the sovereignty, owing it no allegiance, and therefore under no obligation to defend it. The African race, however, born in the country, did owe allegiance to the Government, whether they were slave or free; but it is repudiated, and rejected from the duties and obligations of citizenship in marked language.

The third act to which we have alluded is even still more decisive; it was passed as late as 1813, and it provides: "That from and after the termination of the war in which the United States are now engaged with Great Britain, it shall not be lawful to employ, on board of any public or private vessels of the United States, any person or persons except citizens of the United States, *or* persons of color, natives of the United States.

Here the line of distinction is drawn in express words. Persons of color, in the judgment of Congress, were not included in the word citizens, and they are described as another and different class of persons, and authorized to be employed, if born in the United States.

And even as late as 1820, in the charter to the city of Washington, the corporation is authorized "to restrain and prohibit the nightly and other disorderly meetings of slaves, free negroes, and mulattoes," thus associating them together in its legislation; and after prescribing the punishment that may be inflicted on the slaves, proceeds in the following words: "And to punish such free negroes and mulattoes by penalties not exceeding twenty dollars for any one offence; and in case of the inability of any such free negro or mulatto to pay any such penalty and cost thereon, to cause him or her to be confined to labor for any time not exceeding six calendar months." And in a subsequent part of the same section, the act authorizes the corporation "to prescribe the terms and conditions upon which free negroes and mulattoes may reside in the city."

This law, like the laws of the States, shows that this class of persons were governed by special legislation directed expressly to them, and always connected with provisions for the government of slaves, and not with those for the government of free white citizens. And, after such an uniform course of legislation as we have stated, by the colonies, by the States, and by Congress, running through a period of more than a century, it would seem that to call persons thus marked and stigmatized, "citizens" of the United States, "fellow-citizens," a constituent part of the sovereignty, would be an abuse of terms, and not calculated to exalt the character of an American citizen in the eyes of other nations.

. . . . The only two provisions [in the U.S. Constitution] which point to them and include them, treat them as property, and make it the duty of the Government to protect it; no other power, in relation to this race, is to be found in the Constitution; and as it is a Government of special, delegated powers, no authority beyond these two provisions can be constitutionally exercised. The Government of the United States had no right to interfere for any other purpose but that of protecting the rights of the owner, leaving it altogether with the several States to deal with this race, whether emancipated or not, as each State may think justice, humanity, and the interests and safety of society, require. The States evidently intended to reserve this power exclusively to themselves.

No one, we presume, supposes that any change in public opinion or feeling, in relation to this unfortunate race, in the civilized nations of Europe or in this country, should induce the court to give to the words of the Constitution a more liberal construction in their favor than they were intended to bear when the instrument was framed and adopted. Such an argument would be altogether inadmissible in any tribunal called on to interpret it. If any of its provisions are deemed unjust, there is a mode prescribed in the instrument itself by which it may be amended; but while it remains unaltered, it must be construed now as it was understood at the time of its adoption. It is not only the same in words, but the same in meaning, and delegates the same powers to the Government, and reserves and secures the same rights and privileges to the citizen; and as long as it continues to exist in its present form, it speaks not only in the same words, but with the same meaning and intent with which it spoke when it came from the hands of its framers, and was voted on and adopted by the people of the United States. Any other rule of construction would abrogate the judicial character of this court, and make it the mere reflex of the popular opinion or passion of the day. This court was not created by the Constitution for such purposes. Higher and graver trusts have been confided to it, and it must not falter in the path of duty.

What the construction was at that time, we think can hardly admit of doubt. We have the language of the Declaration of Independence and of the Articles of Confederation, in addition to the plain words of the Constitution itself; we have the legislation of the different States, before, about the time, and since, the Constitution was adopted; we have the legislation of Congress, from the time of its adoption to a recent period;

and we have the constant and uniform action of the Executive Department, all concurring together, and leading to the same result. And if anything in relation to the construction of the Constitution can be regarded as settled, it is that which we now give to the word "citizen" and the word "people."

And upon a full and careful consideration of the subject, the court is of opinion, that . . . Dred Scott was not a citizen of Missouri within the meaning of the Constitution of the United States, and not entitled as such to sue in its courts. . . .

[F]or he admits that he and his wife were born slaves, but endeavors to make out his [right] to freedom and citizenship by showing that they were taken by their owner to [Illinois and Wisconsin, then a part of the Louisiana Territory] where slavery could not by law exist, and that they thereby became free, and upon their return to Missouri became citizens of that State.

Now, if the removal of which he speaks did not give them their freedom, then by his own admission he is still a slave; and whatever opinions may be entertained in favor of the citizenship of a free person of the African race, no one supposes that a slave is a citizen of the State or of the United States. If, therefore, the acts done by his owner did not make them free persons, he is still a slave, and certainly incapable of suing in the character of a citizen.

. . . . In considering this part of the controversy, two questions arise: 1. Was he, together with his family, free in Missouri by reason of the stay in the territory of the United States hereinbefore mentioned? And 2. If they were not, is Scott himself free by reason of his removal to

Rock Island, in the State of Illinois, as stated in the above admissions?

. . . . [The Missouri Compromise, the] act of Congress, upon which [Scott] relies, declares that slavery and involuntary servitude, except as a punishment for crime, shall be forever prohibited in all that part of the territory ceded by France, under the name of Louisiana, which lies north of thirty-six degrees thirty minutes north latitude, and not included within the limits of Missouri. . . .

Now, as we have already said in an earlier part of this opinion . . . the right of property in a slave is distinctly and expressly affirmed in the Constitution. The right to traffic in it, like an ordinary article of merchandise and property, was guarantied to the citizens of the United States, in every State that might desire it, for twenty years. And the Government in express terms is pledged to protect it in all future time, if the slave escapes from his owner. This is done in plain words - too plain to be misunderstood. And no word can be found in the Constitution which gives Congress a greater power over slave property, or which entitles property of that kind to less protection than property of any other description. The only power conferred is the power coupled with the duty of guarding and protecting the owner in his rights.

Upon these considerations, it is the opinion of the court that the [Missouri Compromise] which prohibited a citizen from holding and owning property of this kind in the territory of the United States north of the line therein mentioned, is not warranted by the Constitution, and is therefore void; and that neither Dred Scott himself, nor any of his family, were made free by being carried into this territory; even if they had been carried there by the

owner, with the intention of becoming a permanent
resident.

.... Upon the whole, therefore, it is the judgment of this
court, that it appears by the record before us that [Dred
Scott] is not a citizen of Missouri, in the sense in which
that word is used in the Constitution; and that the Circuit
Court of the United States, for that reason, had no
jurisdiction in the case, and could give no judgment in it.
Its judgment for [Sandford] must, consequently, be
reversed, and a mandate [order to the lower Court] issued,
directing the suit to be dismissed for want of jurisdiction.

*Several months after the Supreme Court's Landmark
Slavery Decision John Sanford sold Dred Scott to
abolitionist Taylor Blow, the man who had financed
Scott's legal battle, and on May 26, 1857 Blow freed Scott
from slavery. Dred Scott died a free man in the City of
St. Louis on September 17, 1858.*

WOMEN'S SUFFRAGE

MINOR v. HAPPERSETT

UNITED STATES v. ANTHONY

After the Civil War the Fourteenth and Fifteenth Amendments gave freed black male slaves the right to vote. Women, black and white, were ignored. The Women's Suffrage Movement needed a test case to challenge in the courts their exclusion from these Constitutional rights.

Suffragette Virginia Louisa Minor brought suit in a Missouri Circuit Court against Reese Happersett, the Voter Registrar of St. Louis County, based on his refusal, under Missouri law, to register her as a legal voter. Virginia Minor claimed that the State Constitution and Registration Law, limiting the right to vote to men, was a denial of her rights as a citizen under the Fourteenth and Fifteenth Amendments to the U.S. Constitution.

The Fourteenth, ratified in 1868, stated: "No State shall make or enforce any law which shall abridge the privileges or immunities of the citizens of the United States." The Fifteenth Amendment, ratified in 1870, stated: "The right of the citizens of the United States to vote shall not be denied or abridged by the United States or by any state on account of race, color, or previous condition of servitude."

The suit was filed by her husband, Francis, as Virginia Minor had no right to bring suit in her own name. The Minors lost at trial, lost in an intermediate appellate court, and lost in the State Supreme Court. The U.S. Supreme Court granted a review. Oral arguments were heard in February and a decision announced in March 1875.

The opinion of the court was delivered by Chief Justice Morrison Waite.

The complete text of *Minor v. Happersett* can be found in volume 88 of *United States Reports.*

MINOR v. HAPPERSETT

March 29, 1875

CHIEF JUSTICE MORRISON WAITE: The question is presented in this case, whether, since the adoption of the Fourteenth Amendment, a woman, who is a citizen of the United States and of the State of Missouri, is a voter in that State, notwithstanding the provision of the Constitution and laws of the State, which confine the right of suffrage to men alone. . . .

It is contended that the provisions of the Constitution and laws of the State of Missouri which confine the right of suffrage and registration therefor to men, are in violation of the Constitution of the United States and, therefore, void. The argument is, that as a woman, born or naturalized in the United States and subject to the jurisdiction thereof, is a citizen of the United States and of the State in which she resides, she has the right of suffrage as one of the privileges and immunities of her citizenship, which the State cannot by its laws or Constitution abridge.

There is no doubt that women may be citizens. They are persons, and by the Fourteenth Amendment "All persons born or naturalized in the United States and subject to the jurisdiction thereof" are expressly declared to be "citizens of the United States and of the State wherein they reside."

. . . . [S]ex has never been made one of the elements of citizenship in the United States. In this respect men have never had an advantage over women. The same laws precisely apply to both. The Fourteenth Amendment did not affect the citizenship of women any more than it did of men. In this particular, therefore, the rights of Mrs. Minor do not depend upon the Amendment. She has always been a citizen from her birth, and entitled to all the privileges and immunities of citizenship. The Amendment prohibited the State, of which she is a citizen, from abridging any of her privileges and immunities as a citizen of the United States; but it did not confer citizenship on her. That she had before its adoption.

If the right of suffrage is one of the necessary privileges of a citizen of the United States, then the Constitution and laws of Missouri confining it to men are in violation of the Constitution of the United States, as amended, and consequently void. The direct question is, therefore, presented whether all citizens are necessarily voters.

The Constitution does not define the privileges and immunities of citizens. For that definition we must look elsewhere. In this case we need not determine what they are, but only whether suffrage is necessarily one of them.

. . . . The [Fourteenth] Amendment did not add to the privileges and immunities of a citizen. It simply furnished an additional guaranty for the protection of such as he already had. No new voters were necessarily made by it. Indirectly it may have had that effect, because it may have increased the number of citizens entitled to suffrage under the Constitution and laws of the States, but it operates for this purpose, if at all, through the States and the state laws, and not directly upon the citizen.

It is clear, therefore, we think, that the Constitution has not added the right of suffrage to the privileges and

immunities of citizenship as they existed at the time it
was adopted. . . .

[A]fter the adoption of the Fourteenth Amendment, it
was deemed necessary to adopt a fifteenth, as follows:
"The right of citizens of the United States to vote shall
not be denied or abridged by the United States, or by any
State, on account of race, color or previous condition of
servitude." The Fourteenth Amendment had already
provided that no State should make or enforce any law
which should abridge the privileges or immunities of
citizens of the United States. If suffrage was one of these
privileges or immunities, why amend the Constitution to
prevent its being denied on account of race, etc.? Nothing
is more evident than that the greater must include the less,
and if all were already protected, why go through with
the form of amending the Constitution to protect a part?

. . . . As has been seen, all the citizens of the States were
not invested with the right of suffrage. In all, save
perhaps New Jersey, this right was only bestowed upon
men and not upon all of them. Under these circumstances
it is certainly now too late to contend that a government
is not republican, within the meaning of this guaranty in
the Constitution, because women are not made voters.

The same may be said of the other provisions just quoted.
Women were excluded from suffrage in nearly all the
States by the express provision of their Constitutions and
laws. . . . Nothing less than express language would have
been employed to effect so radical a change. So, also, of
the Amendment which declares that no person shall be
deprived of life, liberty or property without due process
of law, adopted as it was as early as 1791. If suffrage was
intended to be included within its obligations, language

better adapted to express that intent would most certainly
have been employed. The right of suffrage, when
granted, will be protected. He who has it can only be
deprived of it by due process of law, but in order to claim
protection he must first show that he has the right.

. . . . For nearly ninety years the people have acted upon
the idea that the Constitution, when it conferred
citizenship, did not necessarily confer the right of
suffrage. If uniform practice, long continued, can settle
the construction of so important an instrument as the
Constitution of the United States confessedly is, most
certainly it has been done here. Our province is to decide
what the law is, not to declare what it should be.

We have given this case the careful consideration its
importance demands. If the law is wrong, it ought to be
changed; but the power for that is not with us. The
arguments addressed to us bearing upon such a view of
the subject may, perhaps, be sufficient to induce those
having the power to make the alteration, but they ought
not to be permitted to influence our judgment in
determining the present rights of the parties now
litigating before us. No argument as to woman's need of
suffrage can be considered. We can only act upon her
rights as they exist. It is not for us to look at the hardship
of withholding. Our duty is at an end if we find it is
within the power of a State to withhold.

Being unanimously of the opinion that the Constitution of
the United States does not confer the right of suffrage
upon anyone, and that the Constitutions and laws of the
several States which commit that important trust to men
alone are not necessarily void, *we affirm* [uphold] *the
judgment of the court below.*

Virginia Louise Minor died in 1894. Twenty-six years later, the Nineteenth Amendment to the U.S. Constitution overruled the Landmark Women's Suffrage decision which bore her name and gave all women the right to vote.

Three years prior to the Landmark Women's Suffrage Decision, *Minor v. Happersett,* radical suffragette Susan B. Anthony attempted, and failed in her effort, to bring her own test case (based on the Fourteenth and Fifteenth Amendments) before the U.S. Supreme Court. *United States v. Anthony,* decided in a Federal District Court, is included here for its historical significance.

In November 1872 Susan B. Anthony entered a Rochester, New York polling place and, in direct violation of federal and state law, voted. Anthony was indicted under an 1870 Act of Congress making it illegal for a woman to vote. She was tried in a Federal Court in June 1873. The maximum penalty for knowingly voting in a federal election without the lawful right to vote was a fine of not more than $500 or imprisonment for not more than 3 years.

The complete text of *United States v. Anthony* can be found in volume 24 of *Federal Cases.*

UNITED STATES v. ANTHONY

JUNE 18, 1873

CIRCUIT JUSTICE WARD HUNT delivered the following ruling: The defendant [Susan B. Anthony] is indicted under the act of congress of May 31, 1870, for having voted for a representative in congress, in November, 1872. Among other things, that act makes it an offence for any person knowingly to vote for such representative without having a lawful right to vote. It is charged that [Miss Anthony] thus voted, she not having a right to vote, because she is a woman. [Miss Anthony] insists that she has a right to vote; and that the provision of the [New York State] constitution, limiting the right to vote to persons of the male sex, is in violation of the fourteenth amendment of the constitution of the United States, and is void.

. . . . The fourteenth amendment creates and defines citizenship of the United States. It had long been contended, and had been held by many learned authorities, and had never been judicially decided to the contrary, that there was no such thing as a citizen of the United States, except as that condition arose from citizenship of some state. No mode existed, it was said, of obtaining a citizenship of the United States, except by first becoming a citizen of some state. This question is now at rest. The fourteenth amendment defines and declares who shall be citizens of the United States, to wit, "all persons born or naturalized in the Untied States, and subject to the jurisdiction thereof." The latter qualification was intended to exclude the children of foreign representatives and the like. With this qualification, every person born in the United States or naturalized is declared to be a citizen of the United States and of the state wherein he resides.

After creating and defining citizenship of the United States, the fourteenth amendment provides, that "no state shall make or enforce any law which shall abridge the privileges of immunities of citizens of the United States." This clause is intended to be a protection, not to all our rights, but to our rights as citizens of the United States only; that is, to rights existing or belonging to that condition or capacity. The expression, citizen of a state, used in the previous paragraph, is carefully omitted here.

. . . . The right of voting, or the privilege of voting, is a right or privilege arising under the constitution of the state, and not under the constitution of the United States. The qualifications are different in the different states. Citizenship, age, sex, residence, are variously required in the different states, or may be so. If the right belongs to any particular person, it is because such person is entitled to it by the laws of the state where he offers to exercise it, and not because of citizenship of the United States. If the state of New York should provide that no person should vote until he had reached the age of thirty years, or after he had reached the age of fifty, or that no person having gray hair, or who had not the use of all his limbs, should be entitled to vote, I do not see how it could be held to be a violation of any right derived or held under the constitution of the United States. We might say that such regulations were unjust, tyrannical, unfit for the regulation of an intelligent state; but, if rights of a citizen are thereby violated, they are of that fundamental class, derived from his position as a citizen of the state, and not those limited rights belonging to him as a citizen of the United States. . . .

The United States rights appertaining to this subject are those, first, under article 1 . . . of the United States constitution, which provides, that electors of representatives in congress shall have the qualifications requisite for electors of the most numerous branch of the state legislature; and second, under the fifteenth amendment, which provides, that "the right of citizens of the United States to vote shall not be denied or abridged by the United States, or by any state, on account of race, color, or previous condition of servitude." If the legislature of the state of New York should require a higher qualification in a voter for a representative in congress than is required for a voter for a member of the house of assembly of the state, this would, I conceive, be a violation of a right belonging to a person as a citizen of the United States. That right is in relation to a federal subject or interest, and is guaranteed by the federal constitution. The inability of a state to abridge the right of voting on account of race, color, or previous condition of servitude, arises from a federal guaranty. Its violation would be the denial of a federal right - that is, a right belonging to the claimant as a citizen of the United States. This right, however, exists by virtue of the fifteenth amendment. If the fifteenth amendment had contained the word "sex," the argument of the defendant would have been potent. She would have said, that an attempt by a state to deny the right to vote because one is of a particular sex is expressly prohibited by that amendment. The amendment, however, does not contain that word. It is limited to race, color, or previous condition of servitude. The legislature of the state of New York has seen fit to say, that the franchise of voting shall be limited to the male sex. In saying this, there is, in my judgment, no violation of the letter, or of the spirit, of the fourteenth or of the fifteenth amendment.

This view is assumed in the second section of the fourteenth amendment, which enacts, that, if the right to vote for federal officers is denied by any state to any of the male inhabitants of such state, except for crime, the basis of representation of such state shall be reduced in a proportion specified. Not only does this section assume that the right of male inhabitants to vote was the especial object of its protection, but it assumes and admits the right of a state, notwithstanding the existence of that clause under which the defendant claims to the contrary, to deny to classes or portions of the male inhabitants the right to vote which is allowed to other male inhabitants. The regulation of the suffrage is thereby conceded to the states as a state's right.

. . . . It does not appear that the other judges passed upon that question. The fourteenth amendment gives no right to a woman to vote, and the voting by Miss Anthony was in violation of law.

If she believed she had a right to vote, and voted in reliance upon that belief, does that relieve her from the penalty? It is argued, that the knowledge referred to in the act relates to her knowledge of the illegality of the act, and not to the act of voting; for, it is said, that she must know that she voted. Two principles apply here: First, ignorance of the law excuses no one; second, every person is presumed to understand and to intend the necessary effects of his own acts. Miss Anthony knew that she was a woman, and that the constitution of this state prohibits her from voting. She intended to violate that provision - intended to test it, perhaps, but, certainly, intended to violate it. The necessary effect of her act was to violate it, and this she is presumed to have intended. There was no ignorance of any fact, but, all the facts being known, she undertook to settle a principle in her own person. She takes the risk, and she can not escape the consequences. . . . The principle is the same in the case before us, and in all criminal cases. The precise question now before me has been several times decided . . . that one illegally voting was bound and was assumed to know the law, and that a belief that he had a right to vote gave no defence, if there was no mistake of fact. No system of criminal jurisprudence can be sustained upon any other principle. Assuming that Miss Anthony believed she had a right to vote, that fact constitutes no defence, if, in truth, she had not the right. She voluntarily gave a vote which was illegal, and thus is subject to the penalty of the law.

Upon the foregoing ruling, the counsel for the defendant requested the court to submit the case to the jury on the question of intent, and with the following instructions: (1) If the defendant, at the time of voting, believed that she had a right to vote, and voted in good faith in that belief, she is not guilty of the offence charged. (2) In determining the question whether the defendant did or did not believe that she had a right to vote, the jury may take into consideration, as bearing upon that question, the advice which she received from the counsel to whom she applied, and, also, the fact, that the inspectors of the election considered the question and came to the conclusion that she had a right to vote. (3) The jury have a right to find a general verdict of guilty or not guilty, as they shall believe that the defendant has or has not committed the offence described in the statute.

The Court declined to submit the case to the jury, on any question, and directed the jury to find a verdict of guilty. A request, by the defendant's counsel, that the jury be polled, was denied by the Court, and a verdict of guilty was recorded. On a subsequent day, a motion for a new trial was made, on the part of the defendant. . . .

Circuit Justice Hunt, in denying the motion, said: The whole law of the case has been reargued, and I have given the best consideration in my power to the arguments presented. . . .

[T]he court had decided, as matter of law, that Miss Anthony was not a legal voter. It had also decided, as matter of law, that, knowing every fact in the case, and intending to do just what she did, she had knowingly voted, not having a right to vote, and that her belief did not affect the question. Every fact in the case was undisputed. There was no inference to be drawn or point made on the facts, that could, by possibility, alter the result. It was, therefore, not only the right, but it seem to me . . . the plain duty of the judge to direct a verdict of guilty. The motion for a new trial is denied.

Federal Circuit Judge Ward Hunt, who, it is said, wrote his opinion before the trial, found Susan B. Anthony guilty as charged and fined her $100. Anthony refused to pay the fine, daring the judge to jail her. To prevent Anthony from appealing her imprisonment to the U.S. Supreme Court, Judge Hunt ignored her failure to pay and the case was closed.

President Grant placed Judge Hunt on the U.S. Supreme Court in 1873. Susan B. Anthony died in 1906. The $100 was never paid.

JAPANESE AMERICAN CONCENTRATION CAMPS

KOREMATSU v. UNITED STATES

Three months after the Japanese Empire's surprise attack on Pearl Harbor, the United States military was authorized by President Franklin Roosevelt's Executive Order No. 9066 and the United States Congress' Act of March 21, 1942 to exclude American citizens of Japanese descent from living in certain areas of the West Coast of the United States.

Several Japanese Americans fought the government in the Courts over these violations of their constitutional protections. Gordon Kiyoshi Hirabayashi challenged the constitutionality of the government-enforced curfew as beyond the war powers of Congress. Hirabayashi lost in the Supreme Court on the basis that the government could take steps it felt necessary to prevent espionage and sabotage in areas threatened by Japanese attack.

Fred Toyosaburo Korematsu fought his exclusion from his home and relocation to a military detention center on the basis that the *Hirabayashi* decision was wrong. He was arrested, tried, and convicted for remaining in San Leandro, California, a "Military Area," contrary to Civilian Exclusion Order No. 34; this order was based on the Executive Order and the Act of Congress, which excluded all persons of Japanese ancestry from that area after May 9, 1942 and placed them involuntarily in relocation camps.

Korematsu's conviction in Federal District Court was upheld by a Federal Appeals Court. The Supreme Court agreed to a review. The case was argued in October 1944 and a decision was announced in December.

The opinion of the Court was delivered by Justice Black.

The complete text of *Korematsu v. United States* appears in volume 323 of *United States Reports.*

KOREMATSU v. UNITED STATES

DECEMBER 18, 1944

JUSTICE HUGO BLACK: The petitioner [Fred Toyosaburo Korematsu], an American citizen of Japanese descent, was convicted in a federal district court for remaining in San Leandro, California, a "Military Area," contrary to Civilian Exclusion Order No. 34 of the Commanding General of the Western Command, U.S. Army, which directed that after May 9, 1942, all persons of Japanese ancestry should be excluded from that area. No question was raised as to [Korematsu]'s loyalty to the United States. . . .

It should be noted, to begin with, that all legal restrictions which curtail the civil rights of a single racial group are immediately suspect. That is not to say that all such restrictions are unconstitutional. It is to say that courts must subject them to the most rigid scrutiny. Pressing public necessity may sometimes justify the existence of such restrictions; racial antagonism never can.

In [this] case prosecution of [Korematsu] was begun by [the obtaining of] information charging violation of an Act of Congress, of March 21, 1942, which provides that " . . . whoever shall enter, remain in, leave, or commit any act in any military area or military zone prescribed, under the authority of an Executive order of the President, by the Secretary of War, or by any military commander designated by the Secretary of War, contrary to the restrictions applicable to any such area or zone or contrary to the order of the Secretary of War or any such military commander, shall, if it appears that he knew or should have known of the existence and extent of the restrictions or order and that his act was in violation thereof, be guilty of a misdemeanor and upon conviction shall be liable to a fine of not to exceed $5,000 or to imprisonment for not more than one year, or both, for each offense."

Exclusion Order No. 34, which [Korematsu] knowingly and admittedly violated, was one of a number of military orders and proclamations, all of which were substantially based upon Executive Order No. 9066. That order, issued after we were at war with Japan, declared that "the successful prosecution of the war requires every possible protection against espionage and against sabotage to national-defense material, national-defense premises, and national-defense utilities. . . ."

One of the series of orders and proclamations, a curfew order . . . subjected all persons of Japanese ancestry in prescribed West Coast military areas to remain in their residences from 8 p.m. to 6 a.m. . . . [T]hat . . . curfew order was designed as a "protection against espionage and against sabotage." In *Hirabayashi v. United States*, we sustained [supported] a conviction obtained for violation of the curfew order. The *Hirabayashi* conviction and this one thus rest on the same 1942 Congressional Act and the same basic executive and military orders, all of which orders were aimed at the twin dangers of espionage and sabotage.

The 1942 Act was attacked in the *Hirabayashi* Case as an unconstitutional delegation of power; it was contended that the curfew order and other orders on which it rested were beyond the war powers of the Congress, the military authorities and of the President, as Commander in Chief of the Army; and finally that to apply the curfew order against none but citizens of Japanese ancestry amounted to a constitutionally prohibited discrimination solely on account of race. To these questions, we gave the serious consideration which their importance justified. We upheld the curfew order as an exercise of the power of the government to take steps necessary to prevent espionage and sabotage in an area threatened by Japanese attack.

In the light of the principles we announced in the *Hirabayashi* Case, we are unable to conclude that it was beyond the war power of Congress and the Executive to exclude those of Japanese ancestry from the West Coast war area at the time they did. True, exclusion from the area in which one's home is located is a far greater deprivation than constant confinement to the home from 8 p.m. to 6 a.m. Nothing short of apprehension by the proper military authorities of the gravest imminent danger to the public safety can constitutionally justify either. But exclusion from a threatened area, no less than curfew, has a definite and close relationship to the prevention of espionage and sabotage. The military authorities, charged with the primary responsibility of defending our shores, concluded that curfew provided inadequate protection and ordered exclusion. They did so, as pointed out in our *Hirabayashi* opinion, in accordance with congressional authority to the military to say who should, and who should not, remain in the threatened areas.

In this case [Korematsu] challenges the assumptions upon which we rested our conclusions in the *Hirabayashi* Case. He also urges that by May 1942, when Order No. 34 was promulgated, all danger of Japanese invastion of the West Coast had disappeared. After careful consideration of these contentions we are compelled to reject them.

Here, as in the *Hirabayashi* Case, "we cannot reject as unfounded the judgment of the military authorities and of Congress that there were disloyal members of that population, whose number and strength could not be precisely and quickly ascertained. We cannot say that the war-making branches of the Government did not have ground for believing that in a critical hour such persons could not readily be isolated and separately dealt with, and constituted a menace to the national defense and safety, which demanded that prompt and adequate measures be taken to guard against it."

Like curfew, exclusion of those of Japanese origin was deemed necessary because of the presence of an unascertained number of disloyal members of the group, most of whom we have no doubt were loyal to this country. It was because we could not reject the finding of the military authorities that it was impossible to bring about an immediate segregation of the disloyal from the loyal that we sustained the validity of the curfew order as applying to the whole group. In [this] case, temporary exclusion of the entire group was rested by the military on the same ground. The judgment that exclusion of the whole group was for the same reason a military imperative answers the contention that the exclusion was in the nature of group punishment based on antagonism to those of Japanese origin. That there were members of the group who retained loyalties to Japan has been confirmed by investigations made subsequent to the exclusion. Approximately five thousand American citizens of Japanese ancestry refused to swear unqualified allegiance to the United States and to renounce allegiance to the Japanese Emperor, and several thousand evacuees requested repatriation to Japan.

We uphold the exclusion order as of the time it was made and when [Korematsu] violated it. In doing so, we are not unmindful of the hardships imposed by it upon a large group of American citizens. But hardships are part of war, and war is an aggregation of hardships. All citizens alike, both in and out of uniform, feel the impact of war in greater or lesser measure. Citizenship has its responsibilities as well as its privileges, and in time of war the burden is always heavier. Compulsory exclusion of large groups of citizens from their homes, except under circumstances of direst emergency and peril, is inconsistent with our basic governmental institutions. But when under conditions of modern warfare our shores are threatened by hostile forces, the power to protect must be commensurate with the threatened danger.

It is argued that on May 30, 1942, the date [Korematsu] was charged with remaining in the prohibited area, there were conflicting orders outstanding, forbidding him both to leave the area and to remain there. Of course, a person cannot be convicted for doing the very thing which it is a crime to fail to do. But the outstanding orders here contained no such contradictory commands.

There was an order issued March 27, 1942, which prohibited [Korematsu] and others of Japanese ancestry from leaving the area, but its effect was specifically limited in time "until and to the extent that a future proclamation or order should so permit or direct." That "future order," the one for violation of which [Korematsu] was convicted, was issued May 3, 1942, and

it did "direct" exclusion from the area of all persons of
Japanese ancestry, before 12 o'clock noon, May 9;
furthermore it contained a warning that all such persons
found in the prohibited area would be liable to
punishment under the March 21, 1942 Act of Congress.
Consequently, the only order in effect touching the
[Korematsu]'s being in the area on May 30, 1942, the date
specified in the information against him, was the May 3
order which prohibited his remaining there, and it was
that same order, which he stipulated in his trial that he
had violated, knowing of its existence. There is therefore
no basis for the argument that on May 30, 1942, he was
subject to punishment, under the March 27 and May 3
orders, whether he remained in or left the area.

It does appear, however, that on May 9, the effective date
of the exclusion order, the military authorities had already
determined that the evacuation should be effected by
assembling together and placing under guard all those of
Japanese ancestry, at central points, designated as
"assembly centers," in order "to insure the orderly
evacuation and resettlement of Japanese voluntarily
migrating from military area No. 1 to restrict and regulate
such migration." And on May 19, 1942, eleven days
before the time petitioner was charged with unlawfully
remaining in the area, Civilian Restrictive Order No. 1
provided for detention of those of Japanese ancestry in
assembly or relocation centers. It is now argued that the
validity of the exclusion order cannot be considered apart
from the orders requiring him, after departure from the
area, to report and to remain in an assembly or relocation
center. The contention is that we must treat these
separate orders as one and inseparable; that, for this
reason, if detention in the assembly or relocation center

would have illegally deprived the petitioner of his liberty, the exclusion order and his conviction under it cannot stand.

We are thus being asked to pass at this time upon the whole subsequent detention program in both assembly and relocation centers, although the only issues framed at the trial related to [Korematsu]'s remaining in the prohibited area in violation of the exclusion order. Had [Korematsu] left the prohibited area and gone to an assembly center we cannot say either as a matter of fact or law, that his presence in that center would have resulted in his detention in a relocation center....

Since [Korematsu] has not been convicted of failing to report or to remain in an assembly or relocation center, we cannot in this case determine the validity of those separate provisions of the order. It is sufficient here for us to pass upon the order which [Korematsu] violated.... It will be time enough to decide the serious constitutional issues which petitioner seeks to raise when an assembly or relocation order is applied or is certain to be applied to him, and we have its terms before us.

Some of the members of the Court are of the view that evacuation and detention in an Assembly Center were inseparable. After May 3, 1942, the date of Exclusion Order No. 34, Korematsu was under compulsion to leave the area not as he would choose but via an Assembly Center. The Assembly Center was conceived as a part of the machinery for group evacuation. The power to exclude includes the power to do it by force if necessary. And any forcible measure must necessarily entail some degree of detention or restraint whatever method of removal is selected. But whichever view is taken, it results in holding that the order under which [Korematsu] was convicted was valid.

It is said that we are dealing here with the case of imprisonment of a citizen in a concentration camp solely because of his ancestry, without evidence or inquiry concerning his loyalty and good disposition towards the United States. Our task would be simple, our duty clear, were this a case involving the imprisonment of a loyal citizen in a concentration camp because of racial prejudice. Regardless of the true nature of the assembly and relocation centers - and we deem it unjustifiable to call them concentration camps with all the ugly connotations that term implies - we are dealing specifically with nothing but an exclusion order. To cast this case into outlines of racial prejudice, without reference to the real military dangers which were presented, merely confuses the issue. Korematsu was not excluded from the Military Area because of hostility to him or his race. He *was* excluded because we are at war with the Japanese Empire, because the properly constituted military authorities feared an invasion of our West Coast and felt constrained to take proper security measures, because they decided that the military urgency of the situation demanded that all citizens of Japanese ancestry be segregated from the West Coast temporarily, and finally, because Congress, reposing its confidence in this time of war in our military leaders - as inevitably it must - determined that they should have the power to do just this. There was evidence of disloyalty on the part of some, the military authorities considered that the need for action was great, and time was short. We cannot - by availing ourselves of the calm perspective of hindsight - now say that at that time these actions were unjustified.

Affirmed.

JUSTICE ROBERT JACKSON, dissenting: Korematsu was born on our soil, of parents born in Japan. The Constitution makes him a citizen of the United States by nativity and a citizen of California by residence. No claim is made that he is not loyal to this country. There is no suggestion that apart from the matter involved here he is not law-abiding and well disposed. Korematsu, however, has been convicted of an act not commonly a crime. It consists merely of being present in the state whereof he is a citizen, near the place where he was born, and where all his life he has lived.

Even more unusual is the series of military orders which made this conduct a crime. They forbid such a one to remain, and they also forbid him to leave. They were so drawn that the only way Korematsu could avoid violation was to give himself up to the military authority. This meant submission to custody, examination, and transportation out of the territory, to be followed by indeterminate confinement in detention camps.

A citizen's presence in the locality, however, was made a crime only if his parents were of Japanese birth. Had Korematsu been one of four - the others being, say, a German alien enemy, an Italian alien enemy, and a citizen of American-born ancestors, convicted of treason but out on parole - only Korematsu's presence would have violated the order. The difference between their innocence and his crime would result, not from anything he did, said, or thought, different than they, but only in that he was born of different racial stock.

Now, if any fundamental assumption underlies our system, it is that guilt is personal and not inheritable. Even if all of one's antecedents had been convicted of treason, the Constitution forbids its penalties to be visited upon him, for it provides that "no attainder of treason shall work corruption of blood, or forfeiture except during the life of the person attainted." But here is an attempt to make an otherwise innocent act a crime merely because this prisoner is the son of parents as to whom he had no choice, and belongs to a race from which there is no way to resign. If Congress in peace-time legislation should enact such a criminal law, I should suppose this Court would refuse to enforce it.

But the "law" which this prisoner is convicted of disregarding is not found in an act of Congress, but in a military order. Neither the Act of Congress nor the Executive Order of the President, nor both together, would afford a basis for this conviction. It rests on the orders of General DeWitt. And it is said that if the military commander had reasonable military grounds for promulgating the orders, they are constitutional and become law, and the Court is required to enforce them. There are several reasons why I cannot subscribe to this doctrine.

It would be impracticable and dangerous idealism to expect or insist that each specific military command in an area of probable operations will conform to conventional tests of constitutionality. When an area is so beset that it must be put under military control at all, the paramount consideration is that its measures be successful, rather than legal. The armed services must protect a society, not merely its Constitution. The very essence of the military job is to marshal physical force, to remove every obstacle to its effectiveness, to give it every strategic advantage. Defense measures will not, and often should not, be held within the limits that bind civil authority in peace. No court can require such a commander in such circumstances to act as a reasonable man; he may be unreasonably cautious and exacting. Perhaps he should be. But a commander in temporarily focusing the life of a community on defense is carrying out a military program; he is not making law in the sense the courts know the term. He issues orders, and they may have a certain authority as military commands, although they may be very bad as constitutional law.

But if we cannot confine military expedients by the Constitution, neither would I distort the Constitution to approve all that the military may deem expedient. That is what the Court appears to be doing, whether consciously or not. I cannot say, from any evidence before me, that the orders of General DeWitt were not reasonably expedient military precautions, nor could I say that they were. But even if they were permissible military procedures, I deny that it follows that they are constitutional. If, as the Court holds, it does follow, then we may as well say that any military order will be constitutional and have done with it.

The limitation under which courts always will labor in examining the necessity for a military order are illustrated by this case. How does the Court know that these orders have a reasonable basis in necessity? No evidence whatever on that subject has been taken by this or any other court. There is sharp controversy as to the credibility of the DeWitt report. So the Court, having no real evidence before it, has no choice but to accept General DeWitt's own unsworn, self-serving statement, untested by any cross-examination, that what he did was reasonable. And thus it will always be when courts try to look into the reasonableness of a military order.

In the very nature of things military decisions are not susceptible of intelligent judicial appraisal. They do not pretend to rest on evidence, but are made on information that often would not be admissible and on assumptions that could not be proved. Information in support of an order could not be disclosed to courts without danger that it would reach the enemy. Neither can courts act on communications made in confidence. Hence courts can never have any real alternative to accepting the mere declaration of the authority that issued the order that it was reasonably necessary from a military viewpoint.

Much is said of the danger to liberty from the Army program for deporting and detaining these citizens of Japanese extraction. But a judicial construction of the due process clause that will sustain this order is a far more subtle blow to liberty than the promulgation of the order itself. A military order, however unconstitutional, is not apt to last longer than the military emergency. Even during that period a succeeding commander may revoke it all. But once a judicial opinion rationalizes such an order to show that it conforms to the Constitution, or rather rationalizes the Constitution to show that the Constitution sanctions such an order, the Court for all time has validated the principle of racial discrimination in criminal procedure and of transplanting American citizens. The principle then lies about like a loaded weapon ready for the hand of any authority that can bring forward a plausible claim of an urgent need. Every repetition imbeds that principle more deeply in our law and thinking and expands it to new purposes. All who observe the work of courts are familiar with what Judge Cardozo described as "the tendency of a principle to expand itself to the limit of its logic." A military commander may overstep the bounds of constitutionality, and it is an incident. But if we review and approve, that passing incident becomes the doctrine of the Constitution. There it has a generative power of its own, and all that it creates will be in its own image. Nothing better illustrates this danger than does the Court's opinion in this case.

It argues that we are bound to uphold the conviction of Korematsu because we upheld one in *Hirabayashi v. United States*, when we sustained these orders in so far as they applied a curfew requirement to a citizen of Japanese ancestry. I think we should learn something from that experience.

In that case we were urged to consider only the curfew feature, that being all that technically was involved, because it was the only count necessary to sustain Hirabayashi's conviction and sentence. We yielded, and the Chief Justice guarded the opinion as carefully as language will do. He said: "Our investigation here does not go beyond the inquiry whether, in the light of all the relevant circumstances preceding and attending their promulgation, the challenged orders and statute *afforded a reasonable basis for the action taken in imposing the curfew*. . . . We decide only the issue as we have defined it - we decide only that the *curfew order* as applied, and at the time it was applied, was within the boundaries of the war power." And again: "It is unnecessary to consider whether or to what extent *such findings would support orders differing from the curfew order*." However, in spite of our limiting words we did validate a discrimination on the basis of ancestry for mild and temporary deprivation of liberty. Now the principle of racial discrimination is pushed from support of mild measures to very harsh ones, and from temporary deprivations to indeterminate ones. And the precedent which it is said requires us to do so is *Hirabayashi*. The Court is now saying that in *Hirabayashi* we did decide the very things we there said we were not deciding. Because we said that these citizens could be made to stay in their homes during the hours of dark, it is said we must require them to leave home entirely; and if that, we are told they may also be taken into custody for deportation; and if that, it is argued they may also be held for some undetermined time in detention camps. How far the principle of this case would be extended before plausible reasons would play out, I do not know.

I should hold that a civil court cannot be made to enforce an order which violates constitutional limitations even if it is a reasonable exercise of military authority. The courts can exercise only the judicial power, can apply only law, and must abide by the Constitution, or they cease to be civil courts and become instruments of military policy.

Of course the existence of a military power resting on force, so vagrant, so centralized, so necessarily heedless of the individual, is an inherent threat to liberty. But I would not lead people to rely on this Court for a review that seems to me wholly delusive. The military reasonableness of these orders can only be determined by military superiors. If the people ever let command of the war power fall into irresponsible and unscrupulous hands, the courts wield no power equal to its restraint. The chief restraint upon those who command the physical forces of the country, in the future as in the past, must be their responsibility to the political judgments of their contemporaries and to the moral judgments of history.

My duties as a justice as I see them do not require me to make a military judgment as to whether General DeWitt's evacuation and detention program was a reasonable military necessity. I do not suggest that the courts should have attempted to interfere with the Army in carrying out its task. But I do not think they may be asked to execute a military expedient that has no place in law under the Constitution. I would reverse the judgment and discharge the prisoner.

In 1983 the American Civil Liberties Union and the Japanese American Citizens League presented to a United States District Court testimony that the United States government had suppressed evidence in the Korematsu case. U.S. District Court Judge Marilyn Hall Patel vacated the Korematsu conviction.

BIBLE READING
IN THE PUBLIC SCHOOLS

ABINGTON SCHOOL DISTRICT
v. SCHEMPP

In 1958 Edward and Sidney Schempp of Philadelphia, Pennsylvania had all three of their children, Roger, Donna, and Ellory, enrolled in the local public high school, Abington Senior High.

The Commonwealth of Pennsylvania required by law that at the opening of each public school on each school day there be readings, without comment, from the Holy Bible. The passages to be read were selected by the students from the King James, Douay, Revised Standard, or Jewish Holy Scriptures. Participation was voluntary, and students could be excused from the classroom upon written request of their parent or guardian. At Abington Senior High School the Bible readings were followed by a standing recitation of the Lord's Prayer.

The Schempp family, members of the Unitarian Church, contending that the Pennsylvania law violated their First and Fourteenth Amendment rights, brought an action in Federal Court against the School District to halt the practice at Abington and have the Pennsylvania law declared unconstitutional.

A three judge federal court found for the Schempps. The Pennsylvania law was declared to be in violation of the Establishment Clause of the First Amendment as applied to the States by the Fourteenth Amendment. The School District appealed to the Supreme Court and a review was granted in October 1962. Oral arguments were heard in February 1963 and a decision was announced on June 17, 1963.

The opinion of the Court was delivered by Justice Thomas Clark.

The complete text of *Abington School District v. Schempp* can be found in volume 374 of *United States Reports.*

ABINGTON SCHOOL DISTRICT
v. SCHEMPP

JUNE 17, 1963

JUSTICE THOMAS CLARK: Once again we are called upon to consider the scope of the provision of the First Amendment to the United States Constitution which declares that "Congress shall make no law respecting an establishment of religion, or prohibiting the free exercise thereof. . . ." [This case] present[s] the [issue] in the context of state action requiring that schools begin each day with readings from the Bible. . . . In light of the history of the First Amendment and of our [previous decisions] interpreting and applying its requirements, we hold that the practices at issue and the laws requiring them are unconstitutional under the Establishment Clause, as applied to the States through the Fourteenth Amendment.

The Commonwealth of Pennsylvania by law requires that "At least ten verses from the Holy Bible shall be read, without comment, at the opening of each public school on each school day. Any child shall be excused from such Bible reading, or attending such Bible reading, upon the written request of his parent or guardian." The Schempp family, husband and wife and two of their three children, brought suit to enjoin [stop] enforcement of the statute, contending that their rights under the Fourteenth Amendment to the Constitution of the United States are, have been, and will continue to be violated unless this statute be declared unconstitutional as violative of these provisions of the First Amendment. They sought to [stop] the . . . school district, [where] the Schempp children

attend school, and its officers and the Superintendent of
Public Instruction of the Commonwealth from continuing
to conduct such readings and recitation of the Lord's
Prayer in the public schools of the district pursuant to the
statute. . . .

Edward Lewis Schempp, his wife Sidney, and their
children, Roger and Donna, are of the Unitarian faith and
are members of the Unitarian Church in Germantown,
Philadelphia, Pennsylvania, where they, as well as another
son, Ellory, regularly attend religious services. The latter
was originally a party but having graduated from the
school system . . . was voluntarily dismissed from the
action. The other children attend the Abington Senior
High School. . . .

On each school day at the Abington Senior High School
between 8:15 and 8:30 a.m., while the pupils are attending
their home rooms or advisory sections, opening exercises
are conducted pursuant to the statute. The exercises are
broadcast into each room in the school building through
an intercommunications system and are conducted under
the supervision of a teacher by students attending the
school's radio and television workshop. Selected students
from this course gather each morning in the school's
workshop studio for the exercises, which include readings
by one of the students of 10 verses of the Holy Bible,
broadcast to each room in the building. This is followed
by the recitation of the Lord's Prayer, likewise over the
intercommunications system, but also by the students in
the various classrooms, who are asked to stand and join in
repeating the prayer in unison. The exercises are closed
with the flag salute and such pertinent announcements as
are of interest to the students. Participation in the
opening exercises, as directed by the statute, is voluntary.

The student reading the verses from the Bible may select the passages and read from any version he chooses, although the only copies furnished by the school are the King James version, copies of which were circulated to each teacher by the school district. During the period in which the exercises have been conducted the King James, the Douay and the Revised Standard versions of the Bible have been used, as well as the Jewish Holy Scriptures. There are no prefatory statements, no questions asked or solicited, no comments or explanations made and no interpretations given at or during the exercises. The students and parents are advised that the student may absent himself from the classroom or, should he elect to remain, not participate in the exercises.

It appears from the record that in schools not having an intercommunications system the Bible reading and the recitation of the Lord's Prayer were conducted by the homeroom teacher, who chose the text of the verses and read them herself or had students read them in rotation or by volunteers. This was followed by a standing recitation of the Lord's Prayer, together with the Pledge of Allegiance to the flag by the class in unison and a closing announcement of routine school items of interest.

At the first trial Edward Schempp and the children testified as to specific religious doctrines purveyed by a literal reading of the Bible "which were contrary to the religious beliefs which they held and to their familial teaching." The children testified that all of the doctrines to which they referred were read to them at various times as part of the exercises. Edward Schempp testified at the second trial that he had considered having Roger and Donna excused from attendance at the exercises but decided against it for several reasons, including his belief that the children's relationships with their teachers and classmates would be adversely affected.

. . . . The trial court, in striking down the practices and the statute requiring them, made specific findings of fact that the children's attendance at Abington Senior High School is compulsory and that the practice of reading 10 verses from the Bible is also compelled by law. It also found that:

> "The reading of the verses, even without comment, possesses a devotional and religious character and constitutes in effect a religious observance. The devotional and religious nature of the morning exercises is made all the more apparent by the fact that the Bible reading is followed immediately by a recital in unison by the pupils of the Lord's Prayer. The fact that some pupils, or theoretically all pupils, might be excused from attendance at the exercises does not mitigate the obligatory nature of the ceremony for [the statute] unequivocally requires the exercises to be held every school day in every school in the Commonwealth. The exercises are held in the school buildings and perforce are conducted by and under the authority of the local school authorities and during school sessions. Since the statute requires the reading of the 'Holy Bible,' a Christian document, the practice . . . prefers the Christian religion. The record demonstrates that it was the intention of . . . the Commonwealth . . . to introduce a religious ceremony into the public schools of the Commonwealth."

. . . . It is true that religion has been closely identified with our history and government. As we said in *Engel v. Vitale*, "The history of man is inseparable from the history of religion. And . . . since the beginning of that history many people have devoutly believed that 'More things are wrought by prayer than this world dreams of.'" In *Zorach v. Clauson*, we gave specific recognition to the proposition that "[w]e are a religious people whose institutions presuppose a Supreme Being." The fact that the Founding Fathers believed devotedly that there was a God and that the unalienable rights of man were rooted in Him is clearly evidenced in their writings, from the Mayflower Compact to the Constitution itself. This background is evidenced today in our public life through the continuance in our oaths of office from the Presidency to the Alderman of the final supplication, "So help me God." Likewise each House of the Congress provides through its Chaplain an opening prayer, and the sessions of this Court are declared open by the crier in a short ceremony, the final phrase of which invokes the grace of God. Again, there are such manifestations in our military forces, where those of our citizens who are under the restrictions of military service wish to engage in voluntary worship. Indeed, only last year an official survey of the country indicated that 64% of our people have church membership, while less than 3% profess no religion whatever. It can be truly said, therefore, that today, as in the beginning, our national life reflects a religious people who, in the words of Madison, are "earnestly praying, as . . . in duty bound, that the Supreme Lawgiver of the Universe . . . guide them into every measure which may be worthy of his [blessing. . . .]"

This is not to say, however, that religion has been so identified with our history and government that religious freedom is not likewise as strongly imbedded in our public and private life. Nothing but the most telling of personal experiences in religious persecution suffered by our forebears could have planted our belief in liberty of religious opinion any more deeply in our heritage. It is true that this liberty frequently was not realized by the colonists, but this is readily accountable by their close ties to the Mother Country. However, the views of Madison and Jefferson, preceded by Roger Williams, came to be incorporated not only in the Federal Constitution but likewise in those of most of our States. This freedom to worship was indispensable in a country whose people came from the four quarters of the earth and brought with them a diversity of religious opinion. Today authorities list 83 separate religious bodies, each with membership exceeding 50,000, existing among our people, as well as innumerable smaller groups.

Almost a hundred years ago in *Minor v. Board of Education of Cincinnati*, Judge Alphonso Taft . . . stated the ideal of our people as to religious freedom as one of "absolute equality before the law, of all religious opinions and sects. . . .

"The government is neutral, and, while protecting all, it prefers none. . . ."

Before examining this "neutral" position in which the Establishment and Free Exercise Clauses of the First Amendment place our Government it is well that we discuss the reach of the Amendment under the [case before] this Court.

First, this Court has decisively settled that the First Amendment's mandate that "Congress shall make no law respecting an establishment of religion, or prohibiting the free exercise thereof" has been made wholly applicable to the States by the Fourteenth Amendment. Twenty-three years ago in *Cantwell v. Connecticut*, this Court . . . said:

"The fundamental concept of liberty embodied in that [Fourteenth] Amendment embraces the liberties guaranteed by the First Amendment. The First Amendment declares that Congress shall make no law respecting an establishment of religion or prohibiting the free exercise thereof. The Fourteenth Amendment has rendered the legislatures of the states as incompetent as Congress to enact such laws. . . ."

In a series of cases since *Cantwell* the Court has repeatedly reaffirmed that doctrine, and we do so now.

Second, this Court has rejected unequivocally the contention that the Establishment Clause forbids only governmental preference of one religion over another. Almost 20 years ago in *Everson*, the Court said that "[n]either a state nor the Federal Government can set up a church. Neither can pass laws which aid one religion, aid all religions, or prefer one religion over another." And Justice Jackson, dissenting, agreed:

"There is no answer to the proposition . . . that the effect of the religious freedom Amendment to our Constitution was to take every form of propagation of religion out of the realm of things which could directly or indirectly be made public business and thereby be supported in whole or in part at taxpayers' expense. . . . This freedom was first in the Bill of Rights because it was first in the forefathers' minds; it was set forth in absolute terms, and its strength is its rigidity."

Further, [Justices] Rutledge, Frankfurter, Jackson and Burton, declared:

"The [First] Amendment's purpose was not to strike merely at the official establishment of a single sect, creed or religion, outlawing only a formal relation such as had prevailed in England and some of the colonies. Necessarily it was to uproot all such relationships. But the object was broader than separating church and state in this narrow sense. It was to create a complete and permanent separation of the spheres of religious activity and civil authority by comprehensively forbidding every form of public aid or support for religion."

The same conclusion has been firmly maintained ever since that time, and we reaffirm it now.

. . . . Justice Roberts for the Court in *Cantwell v. Connecticut* . . . said . . . "Freedom of conscience and freedom to adhere to such religious organization or form of worship as the individual may choose cannot be restricted by law. On the other hand, it safeguards the free exercise of the chosen form of religion. Thus the [First] Amendment embraces two concepts - freedom to believe and freedom to act. The first is absolute but, in the nature of things, the second cannot be."

A half dozen years later in *Everson v. Board of Education*, this Court, through Justice Black, stated that the "scope of the First Amendment . . . was designed forever to suppress" the establishment of religion or the prohibition of the free exercise thereof. In short, the Court held that the Amendment "requires the state to be a neutral in its relations with groups of religious believers and non-believers; it does not require the state to be their adversary. State power is no more to be used so as to handicap religions than it is to favor them."

And Justice Jackson, in dissent, declared that public schools are organized "on the premise that secular education can be isolated from all religious teaching so that the school can inculcate all needed temporal knowledge and also maintain a strict and lofty neutrality as to religion. The assumption is that after the individual has been instructed in worldly wisdom he will be better fitted to choose his religion."

Moreover, all of the four dissenters, speaking through Justice Rutledge, agreed that "Our constitutional policy ... does not deny the value or the necessity for religious training, teaching or observance. Rather it secures their free exercise. But to that end it does deny that the state can undertake or sustain them in any form or degree. For this reason the sphere of religious activity, as distinguished from the secular intellectual liberties, has been given the two fold protection and, as the state cannot forbid, neither can it perform or aid in performing the religious function. The dual prohibition makes that function altogether private."

.... [I]n 1961 in *McGowan v. Maryland* ... Chief Justice Warren ... said:

"But, the First Amendment, in its final form, did not simply bar a congressional enactment

*establishing a church; it forbade all laws
respecting an establishment of religion.* Thus,
this Court has given the Amendment a 'broad
interpretation . . . in the light of its history and
the evils it was designed forever to suppress. . . .'"

And Justice Black . . . in *Torcaso* [v. Watkins] . . . used
this language:

"We repeat and again reaffirm that neither a
State nor the Federal Government can
constitutionally force a person 'to profess a belief
or disbelief in any religion.' Neither can
constitutionally pass laws or impose requirements
which aid all religions as against non-believers,
and neither can aid those religions based on a
belief in the existence of God as against those
religions founded on different beliefs."

Finally, in *Engel v. Vitale*, only last year, these principles
were so universally recognized that the Court without the
citation of a single case and over the sole dissent of
Justice Stewart, reaffirmed them. The Court found the
22-word prayer used in "New York's program of daily
classroom invocation of God's blessings as prescribed in
the Regents' prayer . . . [to be] a religious activity." It
held that "it is no part of the business of government to
compose official prayers for any group of the American
people to recite as a part of a religious program carried on
by government."

. . . . And in further elaboration the Court found that the
"first and most immediate purpose [of the Establishment
Clause] rested on the belief that a union of government
and religion tends to destroy government and to degrade

religion." When government, the Court said, allies itself
with one particular form of religion, the inevitable result
is that it incurs "the hatred, disrespect and even contempt
of those who held contrary beliefs."

The wholesome "neutrality" of which this Court's cases
speak thus stems from a recognition of the teachings of
history that powerful sects or groups might bring about a
fusion of governmental and religious functions or a
concert or dependency of one upon the other to the end
that official support of the State or Federal Government
would be placed behind the tenets of one or of all
orthodoxies. This the Establishment Clause prohibits.
And a further reason for neutrality is found in the Free
Exercise Clause, which recognizes the value of religious
training, teaching and observance and, more particularly,
the right of every person to freely choose his own course
with reference thereto, free of any compulsion from the
state. This the Free Exercise Clause guarantees. Thus, as
we have seen, the two clauses may overlap. . . . [T]o
withstand the strictures of the Establishment Clause there
must be a secular legislative purpose and a primary effect
that neither advances nor inhibits religion. The Free
Exercise Clause . . . withdraws from legislative power,
state and federal, the exertion of any restraint on the free
exercise of religion. Its purpose is to secure religious
liberty in the individual by prohibiting any invasions
thereof by civil authority. Hence it is necessary in a free
exercise case for one to show the coercive effect of the
enactment as it operates against him in the practice of his
religion. The distinction between the two clauses is
apparent - a violation of the Free Exercise Clause is
predicated on coercion while the Establishment Clause
violation need not be so attended.

Applying the Establishment Clause principles to [this case] we find that [Pennsylvania is] requiring the selection and reading at the opening of the school day of verses from the Holy Bible and the recitation of the Lord's Prayer by the students in unison. These exercises are prescribed as part of the curricular activities of students who are required by law to attend school. They are held in the school buildings under the supervision and with the participation of teachers employed in those schools. . . . The trial court . . . has found that such an opening exercise is a religious ceremony and was intended by the State to be so. We agree with the trial court's finding as to the religious character of the exercises. Given that finding, the exercises and the law requiring them are in violation of the Establishment Clause.

. . . . The conclusion follows that . . . the [law] require[s] religious exercises and such exercises are being conducted in direct violation of the rights of the [Schempps]. Nor are these required exercises mitigated by the fact that students may absent themselves upon parental request, for that fact furnishes no defense to a claim of unconstitutionality under the Establishment Clause. Further, it is no defense to urge that the religious practices here may be relatively minor encroachments on the First Amendment. The breach of neutrality that is today a trickling stream may all too soon become a raging torrent and, in the words of Madison, "it is proper to take alarm at the first experiment on our liberties."

It is insisted that unless these religious exercises are permitted a "religion of secularism" is established in the schools. We agree of course that the State may not establish a "religion of secularism" in the sense of affirmatively opposing or showing hostility to religion, thus "preferring those who believe in no religion over those who do believe." We do not agree, however, that this decision in any sense has that effect. In addition, it might well be said that one's education is not complete without a study of comparative religion or the history of religion and its relationship to the advancement of civilization. It certainly may be said that the Bible is worthy of study for its literary and historic qualities. Nothing we have said here indicates that such study of the Bible or of religion, when presented objectively as part of a secular program of education, may not be effected consistently with the First Amendment. But the exercise . . . [is a] religious [exercise], required by the [State] in violation of the command of the First Amendment that the Government maintain strict neutrality, neither aiding nor opposing religion.

Finally, we cannot accept that the concept of neutrality, which does not permit a State to require a religious exercise even with the consent of the majority of those affected, collides with the majority's right to free exercise of religion. While the Free Exercise Clause clearly prohibits the use of state action to deny the rights of free exercise to *anyone*, it has never meant that a majority could use the machinery of the State to practice its beliefs. Such a contention was effectively answered by Justice Jackson for the Court in *West Virginia State Board of Education v. Barnett*

"The very purpose of a Bill of Rights was to withdraw certain subjects from the vicissitudes of political controversy, to place them beyond the reach of majorities and officials and to establish them as legal principles to be applied by the courts. One's right to . . . freedom of worship . . .

and other fundamental rights may not be
submitted to vote; they depend on the outcome of
no elections."

The place of religion in our society is an exalted one,
achieved through a long tradition of reliance on the home,
the church and the inviolable citadel of the individual
heart and mind. We have come to recognize through
bitter experience that it is not within the power of
government to invade that citadel, whether its purpose or
effect be to aid or oppose, to advance or retard. In the
relationship between man and religion, the State is firmly
committed to a position of neutrality. Though the
application of that rule requires interpretation of a
delicate sort, the rule itself is clearly and concisely stated
in the words of the First Amendment. Applying that rule
to [this case], we affirm the judgment. . . .

It is so ordered.

THE BOOK BANNED IN BOSTON

"FANNY HILL" v. MASSACHUSETTS

The erotic novel *Fanny Hill: Memoirs of a Woman of Pleasure* by Englishman John Cleland was first published about 1750. Two hundred and fifteen years later, in 1965, the Attorney General of Massachusetts, believing the book to be obscene, put on trial not the publisher or distributor, but the book itself, in an attempt to ban its sale.

A Boston Superior Court Justice received *Fanny Hill* into evidence and portions were read into the record. The prosecution and defense both called upon expert testimony relating to the book's literary, historical, and social value. In the end, the trial court judged the book to be obscene according to the laws of the Commonwealth of Massachusetts and ordered the total suppression of the book, declaring it to be "without the protection of the First and Fourteenth Amendments to the Constitution of the United States. . . ."

In 1957 the U.S. Supreme Court had established the *Roth* definition of obscenity, part of which said that to be judged obscene a work must be utterly without redeeming social importance. The Massachusetts Supreme Judicial Court, in upholding the obscenity decision for *Fanny Hill*, stated: "We do not interpret the 'social importance' test as requiring that a book which appeals to prurient interest and is patently offensive must be unqualifiedly worthless before it can be deemed obscene." On the basis of that difference, the case was appealed to and accepted for review by the U.S. Supreme Court.

Oral arguments were heard in December 1965 and a decision was announced on March 21, 1966. The opinion of the Court was delivered by Justice Brennan, joined by Chief Justice Warren and Justice Fortas.

The complete text of *Fanny Hill v. Massachusetts* can be found in volume 383 of *United States Reports.*

"FANNY HILL" v.
MASSACHUSETTS

March 21, 1966

JUSTICE WILLIAM BRENNAN: This is an obscenity case in which *Memoirs of a Woman of Pleasure* (commonly known as *Fanny Hill*), written by John Cleland in about 1750, was [judged] obscene in a proceeding that put on trial the book itself, and not its publisher or distributor. The proceeding was . . . brought by the Attorney General of Massachusetts, pursuant to General Laws of Massachusetts, to have the book declared obscene. [Massachusetts law] requires that the petition commencing the suit be "directed against [the] book by name" and that an order to show cause "why said book should not be judicially determined to be obscene" be published in a daily newspaper and sent by registered mail "to all persons interested in the publication." Publication of the order in this case occurred in a Boston daily newspaper, and a copy of the order was sent by registered mail to G.P. Putnam's Sons, alleged to be the publisher and copyright holder of the book.

. . . G.P. Putnam's Sons intervened in the proceedings in behalf of the book, but it did not claim the right provided . . . to have the issue of obscenity tried by a jury. At the hearing before a justice of the Superior Court . . . the court received the book in evidence and also . . . heard the testimony of experts and accepted other evidence, such as book reviews, in order to assess the literary, cultural, or educational character of the book. This constituted the entire evidence, as neither side availed itself of the opportunity . . . to introduce evidence "as to the manner and form of its publication, advertisement, and distribution." The trial justice [found] *Memoirs* obscene and declared that the book "is not entitled to the protection of the First and Fourteenth Amendments to the Constitution of the United States. . . . The Massachusetts Supreme Judicial Court [agreed]. We [agreed to hear the case].

The term "obscene" appearing in the Massachusetts statute has been interpreted by the Supreme Judicial Court to be as expansive as the Constitution permits: the "statute covers all material that is obscene in the constitutional sense." Indeed, the final decree before us equates the finding that *Memoirs* is obscene within the meaning of the statute with the declaration that the book is not entitled to the protection of the First Amendment. Thus the sole question before the state courts was whether *Memoirs* satisfies the test of obscenity established in *Roth v. United States.*

We defined obscenity in *Roth* in the following terms: "[W]hether to the average person, applying contemporary community standards, the dominant theme of the material taken as a whole appeals to prurient interest." Under this definition . . . three elements must coalesce: it must be established that (a) the dominant theme of the material taken as a whole appeals to a prurient interest in sex; (b) the material is patently offensive because it affronts contemporary community standards relating to the description or representation of sexual matters; and (c) the material is utterly without redeeming social value.

The Supreme Judicial Court purported to apply the *Roth* definition of obscenity and held all three criteria satisfied. . . . [R]eversal is required because the court

misinterpreted the social value criterion. The court
applied the criterion in this passage:

> "It remains to consider whether the book can be
> said to be 'utterly without social importance.'
> We are mindful that there was expert testimony,
> much of which was strained, to the effect that
> *Memoirs* is a structural novel with literary merit;
> that the book displays a skill in characterization
> and a gift for comedy; that it plays a part in the
> history of the development of the English novel;
> and that it contains a moral, namely, that sex with
> love is superior to sex in a brothel. But the fact
> that the testimony may indicate this book has
> some minimal literary value does not mean it is
> of any social importance. We do not interpret
> the 'social importance' test as requiring that a
> book which appeals to prurient interest and is
> patently offensive must be unqualifiedly
> worthless before it can be deemed obscene."

The Supreme Judicial Court erred in holding that a book
need not be "unqualifiedly worthless before it can be
deemed obscene." A book cannot be proscribed unless it
is found to be *utterly* without redeeming social value.
This is so even though the book is found to possess the
requisite prurient appeal and to be patently offensive.
Each of the three . . . criteria is to be applied
independently; the social value of the book can neither be
weighed against nor canceled by its prurient appeal or
patent offensiveness. . . .

It does not necessarily follow . . . that a determination that
Memoirs is obscene in the constitutional sense would be

improper under all circumstances. On the premise . . .
that *Memoirs* has the requisite prurient appeal and is
patently offensive, but has only a minimum of social
value, the circumstances of production, sale, and publicity
are relevant in determining whether or not the
publication or distribution of the book is constitutionally
protected. Evidence that the book was commercially
exploited for the sake of prurient appeal, to the exclusion
of all other values, might justify the conclusion that the
book was *utterly* without redeeming social importance. It
is not that in such a setting the social value test is relaxed
so as to dispense with the requirement that a book be
utterly devoid of social value, but rather that . . . where
the purveyor's sole emphasis is on the sexually
provocative aspects of his publications, a court could
accept his evaluation at its face value. In this proceeding,
however, the courts were asked to judge the obscenity of
Memoirs in the abstract, and the declaration of obscenity
was neither aided nor limited by a specific set of
circumstances of production, sale, and publicity. All
possible uses of the book must therefore be considered,
and the mere risk that the book might be exploited by
panderers because it so pervasively treats sexual matters
cannot alter the fact - given the view of the Massachusetts
court attributing to *Memoirs* a modicum of literary and
historical value - that the book will have redeeming social
importance in the hands of those who publish or
distribute it on the basis of that value.

Reversed.

JUSTICE WILLIAM O. DOUGLAS, concurring: Memoirs
of a Woman of Pleasure . . . concededly is an erotic novel.
It was first published in about 1749 and has endured to
this date, despite periodic efforts to suppress it. The book

relates the adventures of a young girl who becomes a prostitute in London. At the end, she abandons that life and marries her first lover. . . .

In 1963, an American publishing house undertook the publication of Memoirs. The record indicates that an unusually large number of orders were placed by universities and libraries; the Library of Congress requested the right to translate the book into Braille. But the Commonwealth of Massachusetts instituted the suit that ultimately found its way here, praying that the book be declared obscene so that the citizens of Massachusetts might be spared the necessity of determining for themselves whether or not to read it.

The courts of Massachusetts found the book "obscene" and upheld its suppression. This Court reverses, the prevailing opinion having seized upon language in the opinion of the Massachusetts Supreme Judicial Court in which it is candidly admitted that Fanny Hill has at least "some minimal literary value." I do not believe that the Court should decide this case on so disingenuous a basis as this. I base my vote to reverse on my view that the First Amendment does not permit the censorship of expression not brigaded with illegal action. But even applying the prevailing view of the Roth test, reversal is compelled by this record which makes clear that Fanny Hill is not "obscene." The prosecution made virtually no effort to prove that this book is "utterly without redeeming social importance." The defense, on the other hand, introduced considerable and impressive testimony to the effect that this was a work of literary, historical, and social importance.

We are judges, not literary experts or historians or philosophers. We are not competent to render an independent judgment as to the worth of this or any other book, except in our capacity as private citizens. . . . If there is to be censorship, the wisdom of experts on such matters as literary merit and historical significance must be evaluated. On this record, the Court has no choice but to reverse the judgment of the Massachusetts Supreme Judicial Court, irrespective of whether we would include Fanny Hill in our own libraries.

Four of the seven Justices of the Massachusetts Supreme Judicial Court conclude that Fanny Hill is obscene. Four of the seven judges of the New York Court of Appeals conclude that it is not obscene. To outlaw the book on such a voting record would be to let majorities rule where minorities were thought to be supreme. The Constitution forbids abridgment of "freedom of speech, or of the press." Censorship is the most notorious form of abridgment. It substitutes majority rule where minority tastes or viewpoints were to be tolerated.

It is to me inexplicable how a book that concededly has social worth can nonetheless be banned because of the manner in which it is advertised and sold. However florid its cover, whatever the pitch of its advertisements, the contents remain the same.

Every time an obscenity case is to be argued here, my office is flooded with letters and postal cards urging me to protect the community or the Nation by striking down the publication. The messages are often identical even down to commas and semicolons. The inference is irresistible that they were all copied from a school or church blackboard. Dozens of postal cards often are

mailed from the same precinct. The drives are incessant
and the pressures are great. Happily we do not bow to
them. I mention them only to emphasize the lack of
popular understanding of our constitutional system.
Publications and utterances were made immune from
majoritarian control by the First Amendment, applicable
to the States by reason of the Fourteenth. No exceptions
were made, not even for obscenity. The Court's contrary
conclusion in *Roth*, where obscenity was found to be
"outside" the First Amendment, is without
justification. . . .

Neither reason nor history warrants exclusion of any
particular class of expression from the protection of the
First Amendment on nothing more than a judgment that
it is utterly without merit. We faced the difficult
questions the First Amendment poses with regard to libel
in *New York Times v. Sullivan*, where we recognized that
"libel can claim no talismanic immunity from
constitutional limitations." We ought not to permit
fictionalized assertions of constitutional history to obscure
those questions here. Were the Court to undertake that
inquiry, it would be unable, in my opinion, to escape the
conclusion that no interest of society with regard to
suppression of "obscene" literature could override the
First Amendment to justify censorship.

The censor is always quick to justify his function in terms
that are protective of society. But the First Amendment,
written in terms that are absolute, deprives the States of
any power to pass on the value, the propriety, or the
morality of a particular expression. Perhaps the most
frequently assigned justification for censorship is the
belief that erotica produce antisocial sexual conduct. But
that relationship has yet to be proven. Indeed, if one were

to make judgments on the basis of speculation, one might guess that literature of the most pornographic sort would, in many cases provide a substitute - not a stimulus - for antisocial sexual conduct. As I read the First Amendment, judges cannot gear the literary diet of an entire nation to whatever tepid stuff is incapable of triggering the most demented mind. The First Amendment demands more than a horrible example or two of the perpetrator of a crime of sexual violence, in whose pocket is found a pornographic book, before it allows the Nation to be saddled with a regime of censorship.

Whatever may be the reach of the power to regulate *conduct*, I stand by my view in *Roth v. United States . . .* that the First Amendment leaves no power in government over *expression of ideas. . . .*

JUSTICE BYRON WHITE, dissenting: In *Roth v. United States*, the Court held a publication to be obscene if its predominant theme appeals to the prurient interest in a manner exceeding customary limits of candor. Material of this kind, the Court said, is "utterly without redeeming social importance" and is therefore unprotected by the First Amendment.

To say that material within the *Roth* definition of obscenity is nevertheless not obscene if it has some redeeming social value is to reject one of the basic propositions of the *Roth* case - that such material is not protected *because* it is inherently and utterly without social value.

If "social importance" is to be used as the prevailing opinion uses it today, obscene material, however far beyond customary limits of candor, is immune if it has any literary style, if it contains any historical references or language characteristic of a bygone day, or even if it is printed or bound in an interesting way. Well written, especially effective obscenity is protected; the poorly written is vulnerable. And why shouldn't the fact that some people buy and read such material prove its "social value"?

. . . [I]f the predominant theme of the book appeals to the prurient interest as stated in *Roth* but the book nevertheless contains here and there a passage descriptive of character, geography or architecture, the book would not be "obscene" under the social importance test. I had thought that *Roth* counseled the contrary: that the character of the book is fixed by its predominant theme and is not altered by the presence of minor themes of a different nature. The *Roth* Court's emphatic reliance on the quotation from *Chaplinsky v. New Hampshire* means nothing less:

"' . . . There are certain well-defined and narrowly limited classes of speech, the prevention and punishment of which have never been thought to raise any Constitutional problem. *These include the lewd and obscene. . . . It has been well observed that such utterances are no essential part of any exposition of ideas, and are of such slight social value as a step to truth that any benefit that may be derived from them is clearly outweighed by the social interest in order and morality. . . .*'"

In my view, "social importance" is not an independent test of obscenity but is relevant only to determining the predominant prurient interest of the material, a determination which the court or the jury will make based on the material itself and all the evidence in the case, expert or otherwise.

Application of the *Roth* test, as I understand it, necessarily involves the exercise of judgment by legislatures, courts and juries. But this does not mean that there are no limits to what may be done in the name of *Roth. Roth* does not mean that legislature is free to ban books simply because they deal with sex or because they appeal to the prurient interest. Nor does it mean that if books like *Fanny Hill* are unprotected, their nonprurient appeal is necessarily lost to the world. Literary style, history, teachings about sex, character description (even of a prostitute) or moral lessons need not come wrapped in such packages. The fact that they do impeaches their claims to immunity from legislative censure.

Finally, it should be remembered that if the publication and sale of *Fanny Hill* and like books are proscribed, it is not the Constitution that imposes the ban. Censure stems from a legislative act, and legislatures are constitutionally free to embrace such books whenever they wish to do so. But if a State insists on treating *Fanny Hill* as obscene and forbidding its sale, the First Amendment does not prevent it from doing so.

I would affirm the judgment [of the Massachusetts Supreme Judicial Court].

RIGHTS OF THE ACCUSED

MIRANDA v. ARIZONA

On March 13, 1963 Ernesto Miranda was arrested in Phoenix, Arizona on suspicion of kidnapping and rape. He was taken in custody to a Phoenix police station where he was positively identified by the victim. Miranda was sent to an interrogation room, where he was questioned for two hours by police officers. He was not informed before his interrogation of his right to remain silent or his right to consult with an attorney. During the interrogation Miranda gave an oral confession to police officers who only then informed him that anything he said in their presence could be used as evidence against him. Miranda then signed a written confession. At the top of the confession was a pretyped waiver stating that the confession was made voluntarily, without threats or promises, and with full knowledge of his legal rights.

At his trial, Miranda recanted his written confession and waiver of rights which, over his lawyer's objection, were entered into evidence. The police officers testified to his oral confession and their post-confession reading of his rights. A jury found Ernesto Miranda guilty of rape and kidnapping and he was sentenced to 20 to 30 years in prison. On appeal, the Arizona Supreme Court held that Miranda's constitutional rights against self-incrimination had not been violated by the police in obtaining his confession. Miranda appealed to the United States Supreme Court for a reversal of his conviction. The Court granted a review. Oral arguments were heard in February and March 1966 and a decision was announced in June.

The opinion of the court was delivered by Chief Justice Earl Warren.

The complete text of *Miranda v. Arizona* can be found in volume 384 of *United States Reports.*

MIRANDA v. ARIZONA

June 13, 1966

CHIEF JUSTICE EARL WARREN: The [case] before us raise[s] questions which go to the roots of our concepts of American criminal jurisprudence: the restraints society must observe consistent with the Federal Constitution in prosecuting individuals for crime. More specifically, we deal with the admissibility of statements obtained from an individual who is subjected to custodial police interrogation and the necessity for procedures which assure that the individual is accorded his privilege under the Fifth Amendment to the Constitution not to be compelled to incriminate himself.

We dealt with certain phases of this problem recently in *Escobedo v. Illinois*. There . . . law enforcement officials took the defendant into custody and interrogated him in a police station for the purpose of obtaining a confession. The police did not effectively advise him of his right to remain silent or of his right to consult with his attorney. Rather, they confronted him with an alleged accomplice who accused him of having perpetrated a murder. When the defendant denied the accusation and said "I didn't shoot Manuel, you did it," they handcuffed him and took him to an interrogation room. There, while handcuffed and standing, he was questioned for four hours until he confessed. During this interrogation, the police denied his request to speak to his attorney, and they prevented his retained attorney, who had come to the police station, from consulting with him. At his trial, the State, over his

objection, introduced the confession against him. We held
that the statements thus made were constitutionally
inadmissible.

This case has been the subject of judicial interpretation
and spirited legal debate since it was decided two years
ago. Both state and federal courts, in assessing its
implications, have arrived at varying conclusions. . . . We
granted certiorari [Supreme Court review] . . . to explore
some facets of the problems . . . of applying the privilege
against self-incrimination to in-custody interrogation, and
to give concrete constitutional guidelines for law
enforcement agencies and courts to follow.

. . . . We have undertaken a thorough re-examination of
the *Escobedo* decision and the principles it announced,
and we reaffirm it. That case was but an explication of
basic rights that are enshrined in our Constitution - that
"No person . . . shall be compelled in any criminal case to
be a witness against himself," and that "the accused shall
. . . have the Assistance of Counsel" - rights which were
put in jeopardy in that case through official overbearing.
These precious rights were fixed in our Constitution only
after centuries of persecution and struggle. And in the
words of Chief Justice Marshall, they were secured "for
ages to come, and . . . designed to approach immortality as
nearly as human institutions can approach it."

Over 70 years ago, our predecessors on this Court
eloquently stated:

    " . . . . While the admissions or confessions of the
    prisoner, when voluntarily and freely made, have
    always ranked high in the scale of incriminating
    evidence, if an accused person be asked to explain

his apparent connection with a crime under investigation, the ease with which the questions put to him may assume an inquisitorial character, the temptation to press the witness unduly, to browbeat him if he be timid or reluctant, to push him into a corner, and to entrap him into fatal contradictions, which is so painfully evident in many . . . earlier state trials . . . made the system so odious as to give rise to a demand for its total abolition. The change in the English criminal procedure in that particular seems to be founded upon . . . a general and silent acquiescence of the courts in a popular demand. But, however adopted, it has become firmly embedded in English, as well as in American jurisprudence. So deeply did the iniquities of the ancient system impress themselves upon the minds of the American colonists that the States, with one accord, made a denial of the right to question an accused person a part of their fundamental law. . . ."

In stating the obligation of the judiciary to apply these constitutional rights, this Court declared in *Weems v. United States*:

" . . . our contemplation cannot be only of what has been but of what may be. . . . Rights declared in words might be lost in reality. And this has been recognized. The meaning and vitality of the Constitution have developed against narrow and restrictive construction."

This was the spirit in which we delineated, in meaningful language, the manner in which the constitutional rights of the individual could be enforced against overzealous police practices. It was necessary in *Escobedo*, as here, to insure that what was proclaimed in the Constitution had not become but a "form of words," in the hands of government officials. And it is in this spirit, consistent with our role as judges, that we adhere to the principles of *Escobedo* today.

Our holding will be spelled out with some specificity in the pages which follow but briefly stated it is this: the prosecution may not use statements, whether exculpatory [clearing of guilt] or inculpatory [incriminating], stemming from custodial interrogation of the defendant unless it demonstrates the use of procedural safeguards effective to secure the privilege against self-incrimination. By custodial interrogation, we mean questioning initiated by law enforcement officers after a person has been taken into custody or otherwise deprived of his freedom of action in any significant way. As for the procedural safeguards to be employed, unless other fully effective means are devised to inform accused persons of their right of silence and to assure a continuous opportunity to exercise it, the following measures are required. Prior to any questioning, the person must be warned that he has a right to remain silent, that any statement he does make may be used as evidence against him, and that he has a right to the presence of an attorney, either retained or appointed. The defendant may waive effectuation of these rights, provided the waiver is made voluntarily, knowingly and intelligently. If, however, he indicates in any manner and at any stage of the process that he wishes to consult with an attorney before speaking there can be no questioning. Likewise, if the individual is alone and indicates in any manner that he does not wish to be interrogated, the police may not question him. The mere fact that he may have answered some questions or volunteered some statements on his own does not deprive him of the right to refrain from answering any further inquiries until he has consulted with an attorney and thereafter consents to be questioned.

The constitutional issue we decide in [this case] is the admissibility of statements obtained from a defendant questioned while in custody or otherwise deprived of his freedom of action in any significant way. . . . [Miranda] was questioned . . . in a room in which he was cut off from the outside world. [Nor] was [he] given a full and effective warning of his rights at the outset of the interrogation process. . . . [T]he questioning elicited [an] oral [admission] . . . which [was] admitted at [trial]. [There was] incommunicado interrogation . . . in a police-dominated atmosphere, resulting in [a] self-incriminating [statement] without full [warning] of constitutional rights.

An understanding of the nature and setting of this in-custody interrogation is essential to our decisions today. The difficulty in depicting what transpires at such interrogations stems from the fact that in this country they have largely taken place incommunicado. From extensive factual studies undertaken in the early 1930's, including the famous Wickersham Report to Congress by a Presidential Commission, it is clear that police violence and the "third degree" flourished at that time. In a series of cases decided by this Court long after these studies, the police resorted to physical brutality - beating, hanging, whipping - and to sustained and protracted questioning incommunicado in order to extort confessions. The Commission on Civil Rights in 1961 found much evidence to indicate that "some policemen still resort to physical force to obtain confessions." The use of physical brutality and violence is not, unfortunately, relegated to the past or to any part of the country. Only recently in Kings County, New York, the police brutally beat, kicked and placed lighted cigarette butts on the back of a potential witness under interrogation for the purpose of securing a statement incriminating a third party.

. . . . Again we stress that the modern practice of in-custody interrogation is psychologically rather than physically oriented. As we have stated before, " . . . [T]his court has recognized that coercion can be mental as well as physical, and that the blood of the accused is not the only hallmark of an unconstitutional inquisition." Interrogation still takes place in privacy. Privacy results in secrecy and this in turn results in a gap in our knowledge as to what in fact goes on in the interrogation rooms. A valuable source of information about present police practices, however, may be found in various police manuals and texts which document procedures employed with success in the past, and which recommend various other effective tactics. These texts are used by law enforcement agencies themselves as guides. It should be noted that these texts professedly present the most enlightened and effective means presently used to obtain statements through custodial interrogation. By considering these texts and other data, it is possible to describe procedures observed and noted around the country.

The officers are told by the manuals that the "principal psychological factor contributing to a successful interrogation is *privacy* - being alone with the person under interrogation." The efficacy of this tactic has been explained as follows:

"If at all practicable, the interrogation should take place in the investigator's office or at least in a room of his own choice. The subject should be deprived of every psychological advantage. In his own home he may be confident, indignant, or recalcitrant. He is more keenly aware of his rights and more reluctant to tell of his indiscretions or criminal behavior within the walls of his home. Moreover his family and other friends are nearby, their presence lending moral support. In his own office, the investigator possesses all the advantages. The atmosphere suggests the invincibility of the forces of the law."

To highlight the isolation and unfamiliar surroundings, the manuals instruct the police to display an air of confidence in the suspect's guilt and from outward appearance to maintain only an interest in confirming certain details. The guilt of the subject is to be posited as a fact. The interrogator should direct his comments toward the reasons why the subject committed the act, rather than court failure by asking the subject whether he did it. Like other men, perhaps the subject has had a bad family life, had an unhappy childhood, had too much to drink, had an unrequited desire for women. The officers are instructed to minimize the moral seriousness of the offense, to cast blame on the victim or on society. These tactics are designed to put the subject in a psychological state where his story is but an elaboration of what the police purport to know already - that he is guilty. Explanations to the contrary are dismissed and discouraged.

The texts thus stress that the major qualities an interrogator should possess are patience and perseverance. One writer describes the efficacy of these characteristics in this manner:

"In the preceding paragraphs emphasis has been placed on kindness and stratagems. The investigator will, however, encounter many situations where the sheer weight of his personality will be the deciding factor. Where emotional appeals and tricks are employed to no avail, he must rely on an oppressive atmosphere of dogged persistence. He must interrogate steadily and without relent, leaving the subject no prospect of surcease. He must dominate his subject and overwhelm him with his inexorable will to obtain the truth. He should interrogate for a spell of several hours pausing only for the subject's necessities in acknowledgment of the need to avoid a charge of duress that can be technically substantiated. In a serious case, the interrogation may continue for days, with the required intervals for food and sleep, but with no respite from the atmosphere of domination. It is possible in this way to induce the subject to talk without resorting to duress or coercion. The method should be used only when the guilt of the subject appears highly probable."

The manuals suggest that the suspect be offered legal excuses for his actions in order to obtain an initial admission of guilt. Where there is a suspected revenge-killing, for example, the interrogator may say:

"Joe, you probably didn't go out looking for this fellow with the purpose of shooting him. My guess is, however, that you expected something from him and that's why you carried a gun - for your own protection. You knew him for what he was, no good. Then when you met him he probably started using foul, abusive language and he gave some indication that he was about to pull a gun on you, and that's when you had to act to save your own life. That's about it, isn't it, Joe?"

Having then obtained the admission of shooting, the interrogator is advised to refer to circumstantial evidence which negates the self-defense explanation. This should enable him to secure the entire story. One text notes that "Even if he fails to do so, the inconsistency between the subject's original denial of the shooting and his present admission of at least doing the shooting will serve to deprive him of a self-defense 'out' at the time of trial."

When the techniques described above prove unavailing, the texts recommend they be alternated with a show of some hostility. One ploy often used has been termed the "friendly-unfriendly" or the "Mutt and Jeff" act:

" . . . In this technique, two agents are employed. Mutt, the relentless investigator, who knows the subject is guilty and is not going to waste any time. He's sent a dozen men away for this crime and he's going to send the subject away for the full term. Jeff, on the other hand, is obviously a kindhearted man. He has a family himself. He has a brother who was involved in a little scrape like this. He disapproves of Mutt and his tactics and will arrange to get him off the case if the

subject will cooperate. He can't hold Mutt off
for very long. The subject would be wise to
make a quick decision. The technique is applied
by having both investigators present while Mutt
acts out his role. Jeff may stand by quietly and
demur at some of Mutt's tactics. When Jeff
makes his plea for cooperation, Mutt is not
present in the room."

The interrogators sometimes are instructed to induce a
confession out of trickery. The technique here is quite
effective in crimes which require identification or which
run in series. In the identification situation, the
interrogator may take a break in his questioning to place
the subject among a group of men in a line-up. "The
witness or complainant (previously coached, if necessary)
studies the line-up and confidently points out the subject
as the guilty party." Then the questioning resumes "as
though there were now no doubt about the guilt of the
subject." A variation on this technique is called the
"reverse line-up":

"The accused is placed in a line-up, but this time
he is identified by several fictitious witnesses or
victims who associated him with different
offenses. It is expected that the subject will
become desperate and confess to the offense
under investigation in order to escape from the
false accusations."

The manuals also contain instructions for police on how
to handle the individual who refuses to discuss the matter
entirely, or who asks for an attorney or relatives. The
examiner is to concede him the right to remain silent.
"This usually has a very undermining effect. First of all,

he is disappointed in his expectation of an unfavorable reaction on the part of the interrogator. Secondly, a concession of this right to remain silent impresses the subject with the apparent fairness of his interrogator." After this psychological conditioning, however, the officer is told to point out the incriminating significance of the suspect's refusal to talk:

> "Joe, you have a right to remain silent. That's your privilege and I'm the last person in the world who'll try to take it away from you. If that's the way you want to leave this, O.K. But let me ask you this. Suppose you were in my shoes and I were in yours and you called me in to ask me about this and I told you, 'I don't want to answer any of your questions.' You'd think I had something to hide, and you'd probably be right in thinking that. That's exactly what I'll have to think about you, and so will everybody else. So let's sit here and talk this whole thing over."

Few will persist in their initial refusal to talk, it is said, if this monologue is employed correctly.

In the event that the subject wishes to speak to a relative or an attorney, the following advice is tendered:

"[T]he interrogator should respond by suggesting that the subject first tell the truth to the interrogator himself rather than get anyone else involved in the matter. If the request is for an attorney, the interrogator may suggest that the subject save himself or his family the expense of any such professional service, particularly if he is innocent of the offense under investigation. The interrogator may also add, 'Joe, I'm only looking for the truth, and if you're telling the truth, that's it.   You can handle this by yourself.'"

From these representative samples of interrogation techniques, the setting prescribed by the manuals and observed in practice becomes clear. In essence, it is this: To be alone with the subject is essential to prevent distraction and to deprive him of any outside support. The aura of confidence in his guilt undermines his will to resist.   He merely confirms the preconceived story the police seek to have him describe.   Patience and persistence, at times relentless questioning, are employed. To obtain a confession, the interrogator must "patiently maneuver himself or his quarry into a position from which the desired objective may be attained."   When normal procedures fail to produce the needed result, the police may resort to deceptive stratagems such as giving false legal advice. It is important to keep the subject off balance, for example, by trading on his insecurity about himself or his surroundings. The police then persuade, trick, or cajole him out of exercising his constitutional rights.

Even without employing brutality, the "third degree" or the specific stratagems described above, the very fact of custodial interrogation exacts a heavy toll on individual liberty and trades on the weakness of individuals. . . .

[T]oday . . . we concern ourselves primarily with this interrogation atmosphere and the evils it can bring. In *Miranda v. Arizona*, the police arrested the defendant and took him to a special interrogation room where they secured a confession. . . .

[T]he defendant was thrust into an unfamiliar atmosphere and run through menacing police interrogation procedures. The potentiality for compulsion is forcefully apparent, for example . . . where the indigent Mexican defendant was a seriously disturbed individual with pronounced sexual fantasies. . . . To be sure, the records do not evince overt physical coercion or patent psychological ploys. The fact remains that . . . the officers [did not] undertake to afford appropriate safeguards at the outset of the interrogation to insure that the statements were truly the product of free choice.

. . . . From the foregoing, we can readily perceive an intimate connection between the privilege against self-incrimination and police custodial questioning. It is fitting to turn to history and precedent [a rule of law established by prior cases] underlying the Self-Incrimination Clause to determine its applicability in this situation.

. . . . [W]e hold that when an individual is taken into custody or otherwise deprived of his freedom by the authorities in any significant way and is subjected to questioning, the privilege against self-incrimination is jeopardized. Procedural safeguards must be employed to protect the privilege, and unless other fully effective means are adopted to notify the person of his right of silence and to assure that the exercise of the right will be scrupulously honored, the following measures are required. He must be warned prior to any questioning that he has the right to remain silent, that anything he says can be used against him in a court of law, that he has the right to the presence of an attorney, and that if he cannot afford an attorney one will be appointed for him prior to any questioning if he so desires. Opportunity to exercise these rights must be afforded to him throughout the interrogation. After such warnings have been given, and such opportunity afforded him, the individual may knowingly and intelligently waive these rights and agree to answer questions or make a statement. But unless and until such warnings and waiver are demonstrated by the prosecution at trial, no evidence obtained as a result of interrogation can be used against him.

A recurrent argument . . . is that society's need for interrogation outweighs the privilege. This argument is not unfamiliar to this Court. The whole thrust of our foregoing discussion demonstrates that the Constitution has prescribed the rights of the individual when confronted with the power of government when it provided in the Fifth Amendment that an individual cannot be compelled to be a witness against himself. That right cannot be abridged. As Justice Brandeis once observed:

"Decency, security and liberty alike demand that government officials shall be subjected to the same rules of conduct that are commands to the citizen. In a government of laws, existence of the government will be imperilled if it fails to observe the law scrupulously. Our Government is the potent, the omnipresent teacher. For good or for ill, it teaches the whole people by its example. Crime is contagious. If the Government becomes a lawbreaker, it breeds contempt for law; it invites every man to become a law unto himself; it invites anarchy. To declare that in the administration of the criminal law the end justifies the means . . . would bring terrible retribution. Against that pernicious doctrine this Court should resolutely set its face."

In this connection, one of our country's distinguished jurists has pointed out: "The quality of a nation's civilization can be largely measured by the methods it uses in the enforcement of its criminal law."

If the individual desires to exercise his privilege, he has the right to do so.   This is not for the authorities to decide.   An attorney may advise his client not to talk to police until he has had an opportunity to investigate the case, or he may wish to be present with his client during any police questioning. In doing so an attorney is merely exercising the good professional judgment he has been taught. This is not cause for considering the attorney a menace to law enforcement. He is merely carrying out what he is sworn to do under his oath - to protect to the extent of his ability the rights of his client. In fulfilling this responsibility the attorney plays a vital role in the administration of criminal justice under our Constitution.

In announcing these principles, we are not unmindful of the burdens which law enforcement officials must bear, often under trying circumstances.   We also fully recognize the obligation of all citizens to aid in enforcing the criminal laws. This Court, while protecting individual rights, has always given ample latitude to law enforcement agencies in the legitimate exercise of their duties. The limits we have placed on the interrogation process should not constitute an undue interference with a proper system of law enforcement. As we have noted, our decision does not in any way preclude police from carrying out their traditional investigatory functions. . . .

Because of the nature of the problem and because of its recurrent significance in numerous cases, we have to this point discussed the relationship of the Fifth Amendment privilege to police interrogation without specific concentration on the facts. . . . We turn now to these facts to consider the application . . . of the constitutional principles discussed above. . . . [W]e have concluded that statements were obtained from the defendant under circumstances that did not meet constitutional standards for protection of the privilege.

. . . . On March 13, 1963, petitioner, Ernesto Miranda, was arrested at his home and taken in custody to a Phoenix police station. He was there identified by the complaining witness. The police then took him to "Interrogation Room No. 2" of the detective bureau. There he was questioned by two police officers. The officers admitted at trial that Miranda was not advised that he had a right to have an attorney present. Two hours later, the officers emerged from the interrogation room with a written confession signed by Miranda. At the top of the statement was a typed paragraph stating that the confession was made voluntarily, without threats or promises of immunity and "with full knowledge of my legal rights, understanding any statement I make may be used against me."

At his trial before a jury, the written confession was admitted into evidence over the objection of defense counsel, and the officers testified to the prior oral confession made by Miranda during the interrogation. Miranda was found guilty of kidnapping and rape. He was sentenced to 20 to 30 years' imprisonment on each count, the sentences to run concurrently. On appeal, the Supreme Court of Arizona held that Miranda's constitutional rights were not violated in obtaining the confession and affirmed [upheld] the conviction. In reaching its decision, the court emphasized heavily the fact that Miranda did not specifically request counsel.

We reverse. From the testimony of the officers and by the admission of [Miranda], it is clear that Miranda was not in any way apprised of his right to consult with an attorney and to have one present during the interrogation, nor was his right not to be compelled to incriminate himself effectively protected in any other manner. Without these warnings the statements were inadmissible. The mere fact that he signed a statement which contained a typed-in clause stating that he had "full knowledge" of his "legal rights" does not approach the knowing and intelligent waiver required to relinquish constitutional rights. . . .

Ernesto Miranda was retried without the confession, convicted on other evidence, and served eight years in prison. In 1976 he was stabbed to death after a card game in a Phoenix bar. The first thing police did when they arrested the accused was read him his Miranda rights.

THE DEATH PENALTY

FURMAN v. GEORGIA

William Henry Furman, a 26-year-old black man with a sixth grade education living in the State of Georgia, shot to death a father of five during a break-in of the family's home. Furman's court-appointed lawyer entered an insanity plea. The Superintendent of the Georgia Central State Hospital, where Furman was committed pending trial, reported that, while mentally deficient, Furman could tell right from wrong and could cooperate in his defense. He was tried for murder, found guilty by a jury, and on September 26, 1968 was sentenced to death.

The Georgia Supreme Court upheld the death sentence. Furman appealed to the U.S. Supreme Court for a reversal on the grounds that the death penalty constituted cruel and unusual punishment in violation of the Eighth and Fourteenth Amendments to the U.S. Constitution. The Supreme Court granted review. The appeal of Furman was heard along with *Jackson v. Georgia* and *Branch v. Texas*, both rape cases in which black defendants were convicted, sentenced to death, and had their death sentences upheld by their State Supreme Courts. Oral arguments were heard in January 1972 and a decision was announced on June 29 of that year.

The opinion of the Court was delivered Per Curiam (by the Court) with five Justices (Douglas, Brennan, Stewart, White, and Marshall) expressing their concurring views.

The complete text of *Furman v. Georgia* appears in volume 408 of *United States Reports.*

FURMAN v. GEORGIA

JUNE 29, 1972

PER CURIAM [by the Court]: Petitioner [Furman] was convicted of murder in Georgia and was sentenced to death pursuant to Georgia [law]. . . . [Review] was granted limited to the following question: "Does the imposition and carrying out of the death penalty . . . constitute cruel and unusual punishment in violation of the Eighth and Fourteenth Amendments?" The Court holds that the imposition and carrying out of the death penalty . . . constitutes cruel and unusual punishment in violation of the Eighth and Fourteenth Amendments. The judgment [of the Georgia Supreme Court] . . . is therefore reversed insofar as it leaves undisturbed the death sentence imposed, and the [case is] remanded [sent back to the Georgia court] for further proceedings.

So ordered.

JUSTICE WILLIAM O. DOUGLAS, concurring: In [Furman v. Georgia] the death penalty was imposed . . . for murder. . . . [T]he determination of whether the penalty should be death or a lighter punishment was left by the State to the discretion of the judge or of the jury. . . . [T]he trial was to a jury. . . . I vote to vacate [set aside the] judgment, believing that the exaction of the death penalty does violate the Eighth and Fourteenth Amendments.

That the requirements of due process ban cruel and unusual punishment is now settled. It [is] also settled that the proscription of cruel and unusual punishments forbids the judicial imposition of them as well as their imposition by the legislature.

Congressman Bingham, in proposing the Fourteenth Amendment, maintained that "the privileges or immunities of citizens of the United States" as protected by the Fourteenth Amendment included protection against "cruel and unusual punishments:" "[M]any instances of State injustice and oppression have already occurred in the State legislation of this Union, of flagrant violations of the guaranteed privileges of citizens of the United States, for which the national Government furnished and could furnish by law no remedy whatever. Contrary to the express letter of your Constitution, 'cruel and unusual punishments' have been inflicted under State laws within this Union upon citizens, not only for crimes committed, but for sacred duty done, for which and against which the Government of the United States had provided no remedy and could provide none."

Whether the privileges and immunities route is followed, or the due process route, the result is the same.

It has been assumed in our decisions that punishment by death is not cruel, unless the manner of execution can be said to be inhuman and barbarous. It is also said . . . that the proscription of cruel and unusual punishments "is not fastened to the obsolete but may acquire meaning as public opinion becomes enlightened by a humane justice." A like statement was made in *Trop v. Dulles* that the Eighth Amendment "must draw its meaning from the evolving standards of decency that mark the progress of a maturing society."

The generality of a law inflicting capital punishment is one thing. What may be said of the validity of a law on the books and what may be done with the law in its application do, or may, lead to quite different conclusions.

It would seem to be incontestable that the death penalty inflicted on one defendant is "unusual" if it discriminates against him by reason of his race, religion, wealth, social position, or class, or if it is imposed under a procedure that gives room for the play of such prejudices.

There is evidence that the provision of the English Bill of Rights of 1689, from which the language of the Eighth Amendment was taken, was concerned primarily with selective or irregular application of harsh penalties and that its aim was to forbid arbitrary and discriminatory penalties of a severe nature:

> "Following the Norman conquest of England in 1066, the old system of penalties, which ensured equality between crime and punishment, suddenly disappeared. By the time systematic judicial records were kept, its demise was almost complete. With the exception of certain grave crimes for which the punishment was death or outlawry, the arbitrary fine was replaced by a discretionary amercement [fine]. Although [the fine]'s discretionary character allowed the circumstances of each case to be taken into account and the level of cash penalties to be decreased or increased accordingly, the [fine] presented an opportunity for excessive or oppressive [penalties].

"The problem of excessive [fines] became so prevalent that three chapters of the Magna Carta were devoted to their regulation...."

The English Bill of Rights, enacted December 16, 1689, stated that "excessive bail ought not to be required, nor excessive fines imposed, nor cruel and unusual punishments inflicted." These were the words chosen for our Eighth Amendment. A like provision had been in Virginia's Constitution of 1776 and in eight other States. The Northwest Ordinance, enacted under the Articles of Confederation, included a prohibition of cruel and unusual punishments. But the debates of the First Congress on the Bill of Rights throw little light on its intended meaning. All that appears is the following:

"Mr. Smith, of South Carolina, objected to the words 'nor cruel and unusual punishments;' the import of them being too indefinite.

"Mr. Livermore: The clause seems to express a great deal of humanity, on which account I have no objection to it; but as it seems to have no meaning in it, I do not think it necessary. What is meant by the terms excessive bail? Who are to be the judges? What is understood by excessive fines? It lies with the court to determine. No cruel and unusual punishment is to be inflicted; it is sometimes necessary to hang a man, villains often deserve whipping, and perhaps having their ears cut off; but are we in the future to be prevented from inflicting these punishments because they are cruel? If a more lenient mode of correcting vice and deterring others from the commission of it could be invented, it would be very prudent in the Legislature to adopt it; but until we have some security that this will be done, we ought not to be restrained from making necessary laws by any declaration of this kind."

The words "cruel and unusual" certainly include penalties that are barbaric. But the words, at least when read in light of the English proscription against selective and irregular use of penalties, suggest that it is "cruel and unusual" to apply the death penalty - or any other penalty - selectively to minorities whose numbers are few, who are outcasts of society, and who are unpopular, but whom society is willing to see suffer though it would not countenance general application of the same penalty across the board. Judge Tuttle indeed made abundantly clear in *Novak v. Beto* that solitary confinement may at times be "cruel and unusual" punishment.

The Court in *McGautha v. California* noted that in this country there was almost from the beginning a "rebellion against the common-law rule imposing a mandatory death sentence on all convicted murderers." The first attempted remedy was to restrict the death penalty to defined offenses such as "premeditated" murder. But juries took "the law into their own hands" and refused to convict on the capital offense.

"In order to meet the problem of jury nullification, legislatures did not try, as before, to refine further the definition of capital homicides. Instead they adopted the method of forthrightly granting juries the discretion which they had been exercising in fact."

The Court concluded: "In light of history, experience, and the present limitations of human knowledge, we find it quite impossible to say that committing to the untrammeled discretion of the jury the power to pronounce life or death in capital cases is offensive to anything in the Constitution."

The Court refused to find constitutional dimensions in the argument that those who exercise their discretion to send a person to death should be given standards by which that discretion should be exercised.

A recent witness before Subcommittee No. 3 of the House Committee on the Judiciary, Ernest van den Haag, stated:

> "Any penalty, a fine, imprisonment or the death penalty could be unfairly or unjustly applied. The vice in this case is not in the penalty but in the process by which it is inflicted. It is unfair to inflict unequal penalties on equally guilty parties, or on any innocent parties, *regardless of what the penalty is.*"

But those who advance that argument overlook *McGautha.*

. . . . Juries (or judges, as the case may be) have practically untrammeled discretion to let an accused live or insist that he die.

Justice Field, dissenting in *O'Neil v. Vermont,* said, "The State may, indeed, make the drinking of one drop of liquor an offence to be punished by imprisonment, but it would be an unheard-of cruelty if it should count the drops in a single glass and make thereby a thousand offences, and thus extend the punishment for drinking the single glass of liquor to an imprisonment of almost indefinite duration." What the legislature may not do for all classes uniformly and systematically, a judge or jury may not do for a class that prejudice sets apart from the community.

There is increasing recognition of the fact that the basic theme of equal protection is implicit in "cruel and unusual" punishments. "A penalty . . . should be considered 'unusually' imposed if it is administered arbitrarily or discriminatorily." The same authors add that "[t]he extreme rarity with which applicable death penalty provisions are put to use raises a strong inference of arbitrariness." The President's Commission on Law Enforcement and Administration of Justice recently concluded:

> "Finally there is evidence that the imposition of the death sentence and the exercise of dispensing power by the courts and the executive follow discriminatory patterns. The death sentence is disproportionately imposed and carried out on the poor, the Negro, and the members of unpopular groups."

A study of capital cases in Texas from 1924 to 1968 reached the following conclusions:

> "Application of the death penalty is unequal: most of those executed were poor, young, and ignorant.

> "Seventy-five of the 460 cases involved codefendants, who, under Texas law, were given separate trials. In several instances where a white and a Negro were co-defendants, the white was

sentenced to life imprisonment or a term of years, and the Negro was given the death penalty.

"Another ethnic disparity is found in the type of sentence imposed for rape. The Negro convicted of rape is far more likely to get the death penalty than a term sentence, whereas whites and Latins are far more likely to get a term sentence than the death penalty."

Warden Lewis E. Lawes of Sing Sing said:

"Not only does capital punishment fail in its justification, but no punishment could be invented with so many inherent defects. It is an unequal punishment in the way it is applied to the rich and to the poor. The defendant of wealth and position never goes to the electric chair or to the gallows. Juries do not intentionally favour the rich, the law is theoretically impartial, but the defendant with ample means is able to have his case presented with every favourable aspect, while the poor defendant often has a lawyer assigned by the court. Sometimes such assignment is considered part of political patronage; usually the lawyer assigned has had no experience whatever in a capital case."

Former Attorney General Ramsey Clark has said, "It is the poor, the sick, the ignorant, the powerless and the hated who are executed." One searches our chronicles in vain for the execution of any member of the affluent strata of this society. The Leopolds and Loebs are given prison terms, not sentenced to death.

.... Furman, a black, killed a householder while seeking to enter the home at night. Furman shot the deceased through a closed door. He was 26 years old and had finished the sixth grade in school. Pending trial he was committed to the Georgia Central State Hospital for a psychiatric examination on his plea of insanity tendered by court-appointed counsel. The superintendent reported that a unanimous staff diagnostic conference on the same date had concluded "that this patient should retain his present diagnosis of Mental Deficiency, Mild to Moderate, with Psychotic Episodes associated with Convulsive Disorder." The physicians agreed that "at present the patient is not psychotic, but he is not capable of cooperating with his counsel in the preparation of his defense"; and the staff believed "that he is in need of further psychiatric hospitalization and treatment."

Later the Superintendent . . . concluded, however, that Furman was "not psychotic at present, knows right from wrong and is able to cooperate with his counsel in preparing his defense."

.... We cannot say . . . that [Furman was] sentenced to death because [he was] black. Yet our task is not restricted to an effort to divine what [motive] impelled [this] death penalt[y]. Rather, we deal with a system of law and of justice that leaves to the uncontrolled discretion of judges or juries the determination whether defendants committing these crimes should die or be imprisoned. Under these laws no standards govern the selection of the penalty. People live or die, dependent on the whim of one man or of 12.

.... Those who wrote the Eighth Amendment knew what price their forebears had paid for a system based, not on equal justice, but on discrimination. In those days the target was not the blacks or the poor, but the dissenters, those who opposed absolutism in government, who struggled for a parliamentary regime, and who opposed government's recurring efforts to foist a particular religion on the people. But the tool of capital punishment was used with vengeance against the opposition and those unpopular with the regime. One cannot read this history without realizing that the desire for equality was reflected in the ban against "cruel and unusual punishments" contained in the Eighth Amendment.

In a Nation committed to equal protection of the laws there is no permissible "caste" aspect of law enforcement. Yet we know that the discretion of judges and juries in imposing the death penalty enables the penalty to be selectively applied, feeding prejudices against the accused if he is poor and despised, lacking political clout, or if he is a member of a suspect or unpopular minority, and saving those who by social position may be in a more protected position. In ancient Hindu law a Brahman was exempt from capital punishment, and in those days, "[g]enerally, in the law books, punishment increased in severity as social status diminished." We have, I fear, taken in practice the same position, partially as a result of making the death penalty discretionary and partially as a result of the ability of the rich to purchase the services of the most respected and most resourceful legal talent in the Nation.

The high service rendered by the "cruel and unusual" punishment clause of the Eighth Amendment is to require legislatures to write penal laws that are evenhanded, nonselective, and nonarbitrary, and to require judges to see to it that general laws are not applied sparsely, selectively, and spottily to unpopular groups.

A law that stated that anyone making more than $50,000 would be exempt from the death penalty would plainly fall, as would a law that in terms said that blacks, those who never went beyond the fifth grade in school, those who made less than $3,000 a year, or those who were unpopular or unstable should be the only people executed. A law which in the overall view reaches that result in practice has no more sanctity than a law which in terms provides the same.

Thus, these discretionary statutes are unconstitutional in their operation. They are pregnant with discrimination and discrimination is an ingredient not compatible with the idea of equal protection of the laws that is implicit in the ban on "cruel and unusual" punishments.

Any law which is nondiscriminatory on its face may be applied in such a way as to violate the Equal Protection Clause of the Fourteenth Amendment. Such consequence might be the adding of a mandatory death penalty where equal or lesser sentences were imposed on the elite, a harsher one on the minorities or members of the lower castes. Whether a mandatory death penalty would otherwise be constitutional is a question I do not reach.

I concur in the judgments of the Court.

JUSTICE LEWIS POWELL with whom The Chief Justice [Burger], and Justices Blackmun and Rehnquist join, dissenting: The Court granted [review] . . . to consider whether the death penalty is any longer a permissible form of punishment. It is the judgment of five Justices that the death penalty, as customarily prescribed and implemented in this country today, offends the constitutional prohibition against cruel and unusual punishments. The reasons for that judgment are stated in five separate opinions, expressing as many separate rationales. In my view, none of these opinions provides a constitutionally adequate foundation for the Court's decision.

The Court rejects as not decisive the clearest evidence that the Framers of the Constitution and the authors of the Fourteenth Amendment believed that those documents posed no barrier to the death penalty. The Court also brushes aside an unbroken line of precedent reaffirming the heretofore virtually unquestioned constitutionality of capital punishment. . . .

The issue in the first capital case in which the Eighth Amendment was invoked, *Wilkerson v. Utah*, was whether carrying out a death sentence by public shooting was cruel and unusual punishment. A unanimous Court upheld that form of execution, noting first that the punishment itself, as distinguished from the mode of its infliction, was "not pretended by the counsel of the prisoner" to be cruel and unusual. The Court went on to hold that:

> "Cruel and unusual punishments are forbidden by the Constitution, but the authorities . . . are quite sufficient to show that the punishment of shooting as a mode of executing the death penalty for the crime of murder in the first degree is not included in that category. . . ."

Eleven years later, in *In re Kemmler*, . . . this Court was called on to decide whether electrocution, which only very recently had been adopted by the New York Legislature as a means of execution, was impermissibly cruel and unusual in violation of the Fourteenth Amendment. . . . The Court drew a clear line between the penalty itself and the mode of its execution:

"Punishments are cruel when they involve torture or a lingering death; but the punishment of death is not cruel, within the meaning of that word as used in the Constitution. It implies there something inhuman and barbarous, something more than the mere extinguishment of life."

More than 50 years later, in *Louisiana [on Behalf of] Francis v. Resweber*, the Court considered a case in which, due to a mechanical malfunction, Louisiana's initial attempt to electrocute a convicted murderer had failed. Petitioner sought to block a second attempt to execute the sentence on the ground that to do so would constitute cruel and unusual punishment. In the plurality opinion written by Justice Reed . . . relief was denied. Again the Court focused on the manner of execution, never questioning the propriety of the death sentence itself.

. . . . On virtually every occasion that any opinion has touched on the question of the constitutionality of the death penalty, it has been asserted affirmatively, or tacitly assumed, that the Constitution does not prohibit the penalty. No Justice of the Court, until today, has dissented from this consistent reading of the Constitution. . . .

Whether one views the question as one of due process or of cruel and unusual punishment, as I do for convenience in this case, the issue is essentially the same. The

fundamental premise upon which either standard is based
is that notions of what constitutes cruel and unusual
punishment or due process do evolve. Neither the
Congress nor any state legislature would today tolerate
pillorying, branding, or cropping or nailing of the ears
- punishments that were in existence during our colonial
era. Should, however, any such punishment be prescribed,
the courts would certainly enjoin its execution. Likewise,
no court would approve any method of implementation of
the death sentence found to involve unnecessary cruelty
in light of presently available alternatives. Similarly,
there may well be a process of evolving attitude with
respect to the application of the death sentence for
particular crimes.

But we are not asked to consider the permissibility of any
of the several methods employed in carrying out the death
sentence. Nor are we asked . . . to determine whether the
penalty might be a grossly excessive punishment for some
specific criminal conduct. . . . Petitioners' principal
argument . . . insists on an unprecedented constitutional
rule of absolute prohibition of capital punishment for any
crime, regardless of its depravity and impact on
society. . . . What they are saying, in effect, is that the
evolutionary process has come suddenly to an end; that
the ultimate wisdom as to the appropriateness of capital
punishment under all circumstances, and for all future
generations, has somehow been revealed.

I come now to consider, subject to the reservations above
expressed, the two justifications most often cited for the
retention of capital punishment. The concept of
retribution - though popular for centuries - is now
criticized as unworthy of a civilized people. Yet this
Court has acknowledged the existence of a retributive

element in criminal sanctions and has never heretofore found it impermissible. . . .

While retribution alone may seem an unworthy justification in a moral sense, its utility in a system of criminal justice requiring public support has long been recognized. . . .

[N]ot infrequently, cases arise that are so shocking or offensive that the public demands the ultimate penalty for the transgressor.

Deterrence is a more appealing justification, although opinions again differ widely. Indeed, the deterrence issue lies at the heart of much of the debate between the abolitionists and retentionists. Statistical studies, based primarily on trends in States that have abolished the penalty, tend to support the view that the death penalty has not been proved to be a superior deterrent. Some dispute the validity of this conclusion, pointing out that the studies do not show that the death penalty has no deterrent effect on any categories of crimes. . . .

. . . . [N]othing in the history of the Cruel and Unusual Punishments Clause indicates that it may properly be utilized by the judiciary to strike down punishments - authorized by legislatures and imposed by juries - in any but the extraordinary case. This Court is not empowered to sit as a court of sentencing review, implementing the personal views of its members on the proper role of penology. To do so is to usurp a function committed to the Legislative Branch and beyond the power and competency of this Court.

It seems to me that the sweeping judicial action undertaken today reflects a basic lack of faith and confidence in the democratic process. Many may regret, as I do, the failure of some legislative bodies to address the capital punishment issue with greater frankness or effectiveness. Many might decry their failure either to abolish the penalty entirely or selectively, or to establish standards for its enforcement. But impatience with the slowness, and even the unresponsiveness, of legislatures is no justification for judicial intrusion upon their historic powers.

William Henry Furman was paroled from prison on April 19, 1984.

HOMOSEXUALITY

BOWERS v. HARDWICK

In August 1982 Michael Hardwick, a self-described practicing homosexual residing in the State of Georgia, was arrested by Atlanta police and charged with violating that state's sodomy law. Sodomy, oral or anal sexual contact, had been a criminal offense in Georgia since 1816. If convicted, Hardwick, charged with committing sodomy with a consenting adult male in the bedroom of his own home, faced up to 20 years in prison.

After a preliminary hearing on the charge, the local District Attorney declined to present the case to the grand jury without further evidence. Michael Hardwick then sued the State of Georgia, in the person of its Attorney General, Michael Bowers, in Federal District Court, challenging the constitutionality of the Georgia sodomy law as it applied to consensual homosexual sodomy.

The U.S. District Court dismissed Hardwick's lawsuit. Hardwick appealed to the U.S. Court of Appeals, which reinstated the lawsuit, holding that the Georgia sodomy law violated Hardwick's fundamental rights to private and intimate association by reason of the Ninth and Fourteenth Amendments to the U.S. Constitution. The Appeals Court sent the Hardwick case back to the District Court for trial. The Attorney General of Georgia, claiming that other Appeals Courts in California and the District of Columbia had arrived at opposite judgments over the same facts, petitioned the U.S. Supreme Court for a reversal. The Court granted review. Oral arguments were heard in March 1986 and a decision was announced in June.

The opinion of the Court was delivered by Justice Byron White.

The complete text of *Bowers v. Hardwick* can be found in volume 478 of *United States Reports.*

BOWERS v. HARDWICK

JUNE 30, 1986

JUSTICE BYRON WHITE: In August 1982, respondent [Michael] Hardwick was charged with violating the Georgia statute criminalizing sodomy by committing that act with another adult male in the bedroom of [Hardwick]'s home. After a preliminary hearing, the District Attorney decided not to present the matter to the grand jury unless further evidence developed.

[Hardwick] then brought suit in the Federal District Court, challenging the constitutionality of the statute insofar as it criminalized consensual sodomy. He asserted that he was a practicing homosexual, that the Georgia sodomy statute, as administered by the defendants, placed him in imminent danger of arrest, and that the statute for several reasons violates the Federal Constitution. . . .

[T]he Court of Appeals for the Eleventh Circuit . . . [held] that the Georgia statute violated [Hardwick]'s fundamental rights because his homosexual activity is a private and intimate association that is beyond the reach of state regulation by reason of the Ninth Amendment and the Due Process Clause of the Fourteenth Amendment. The case was remanded [sent back to the lower (District) court] for trial, at which . . . the State would have to prove that the statute is supported by a compelling interest and is the most narrowly drawn means of achieving that end.

. . . . This case does not require a judgment on whether laws against sodomy between consenting adults in general,

or between homosexuals in particular, are wise or
desirable.   It raises no question about the right or
propriety of state legislative decisions to repeal their laws
that criminalize homosexual sodomy, or of state-court
decisions invalidating those laws on state constitutional
grounds. The issue presented is whether the Federal
Constitution confers a fundamental right upon
homosexuals to engage in sodomy and hence invalidates
the laws of the many States that still make such conduct
illegal and have done so for a very long time. The case
also calls for some judgment about the limits of the
Court's role in carrying out its constitutional mandate.

We first register our disagreement with the Court of
Appeals and with [Hardwick] that the Court's prior cases
have construed the Constitution to confer a right of
privacy that extends to homosexual sodomy and for all
intents and purposes have decided this case. . . .

[Hardwick] would have us announce, as the Court of
Appeals did, a fundamental right to engage in homosexual
sodomy. This we are quite unwilling to do. . . .

Striving to assure itself and the public that announcing
rights not readily identifiable in the Constitution's text
involves much more than the imposition of the Justices'
own choice of values on the States and the Federal
Government, the Court has sought to identify the nature
of the rights qualifying for heightened judicial protection.
In *Palko v. Connecticut* . . . it was said that this category
includes those fundamental liberties that are "implicit in
the concept of ordered liberty," such that "neither liberty
nor justice would exist if [they] were sacrificed." A
different description of fundamental liberties appeared in
Moore v. East Cleveland, where they are characterized as

those liberties that are "deeply rooted in this Nation's history and tradition."

It is obvious to us that neither of these formulations would extend a fundamental right to homosexuals to engage in acts of consensual sodomy. Proscriptions against that conduct have ancient roots. Sodomy was a criminal offense at common law and was forbidden by the laws of the original 13 States when they ratified the Bill of Rights. In 1868, when the Fourteenth Amendment was ratified, all but 5 of the 37 States in the Union had criminal sodomy laws. In fact, until 1961, all 50 States outlawed sodomy, and today, 25 States and the District of Columbia continue to provide criminal penalties for sodomy performed in private and between consenting adults. Against this background, to claim that a right to engage in such conduct is "deeply rooted in this Nation's history and tradition" or "implicit in the concept of ordered liberty" is, at best, facetious.

Nor are we inclined to take a more expansive view of our authority to discover new fundamental rights imbedded in the Due Process Clause. The Court is most vulnerable and comes nearest to illegitimacy when it deals with judge-made constitutional law having little or no cognizable roots in the language or design of the Constitution. That this is so was painfully demonstrated by the face-off between the Executive and the Court in the 1930's, which resulted in the repudiation of much of the substantive gloss that the Court had placed on the Due Process Clauses of the Fifth and Fourteenth Amendments. There should be, therefore, great resistance to expand the substantive reach of those Clauses, particularly if it requires redefining the category of rights deemed to be fundamental. Otherwise, the Judiciary necessarily takes to itself further authority to govern the country without express constitutional authority. The claimed right pressed on us today falls far short of overcoming this resistance.

[Hardwick], however, asserts that the result should be different where the homosexual conduct occurs in the privacy of the home. He relies on *Stanley v. Georgia*, where the Court held that the First Amendment prevents conviction for possessing and reading obscene material in the privacy of one's home: "If the First Amendment means anything, it means that a State has no business telling a man, sitting alone in his house, what books he may read or what films he may watch."

Stanley did protect conduct that would not have been protected outside the home, and it partially prevented the enforcement of state obscenity laws; but the decision was firmly grounded in the First Amendment. The right pressed upon us here has no similar support in the text of the Constitution, and it does not qualify for recognition under the prevailing principles for construing the Fourteenth Amendment. Its limits are also difficult to discern. Plainly enough, otherwise illegal conduct is not always immunized whenever it occurs in the home. Victimless crimes, such as the possession and use of illegal drugs, do not escape the law where they are committed at home. *Stanley* itself recognized that its holding offered no protection for the possession in the home of drugs, firearms, or stolen goods. And if [Hardwick]'s submission is limited to the voluntary sexual conduct between consenting adults, it would be difficult, except by fiat [order], to limit the claimed right to homosexual conduct while leaving exposed to prosecution adultery, incest, and other sexual crimes even though they are committed in the home. We are unwilling to start down that road.

Even if the conduct at issue here is not a fundamental right, [Hardwick] asserts that there must be a rational basis for the law and that there is none in this case other than the presumed belief of a majority of the electorate in Georgia that homosexual sodomy is immoral and unacceptable. This is said to be an inadequate rationale to support the law. The law, however, is constantly based on notions of morality, and if all laws representing essentially moral choices are to be invalidated under the Due Process Clause, the courts will be very busy indeed. Even [Hardwick] makes no such claim, but insists that majority sentiments about the morality of homosexuality should be declared inadequate. We do not agree, and are unpersuaded that the sodomy laws of some 25 States should be invalidated on this basis.

Accordingly, the judgment of the Court of Appeals is reversed.

JUSTICE JOHN PAUL STEVENS, with whom Justices Brennan and Marshall join, dissenting: Like the statute that is challenged in this case, the rationale of the Court's opinion applies equally to the prohibited conduct regardless of whether the parties who engage in it are married or unmarried, or are of the same or different sexes. Sodomy was condemned as an odious and sinful type of behavior during the formative period of the common law. That condemnation was equally damning for heterosexual and homosexual sodomy. Moreover, it provided no special exemption for married couples. The license to cohabit and to produce legitimate offspring simply did not include any permission to engage in sexual conduct that was considered a "crime against nature."

The history of the Georgia statute before us clearly reveals this traditional prohibition of heterosexual, as well as homosexual, sodomy. Indeed, at one point in the 20th century, Georgia's law was construed to permit certain sexual conduct between homosexual women even though such conduct was prohibited between heterosexuals. The history of the statutes cited by the majority as proof for the proposition that sodomy is not constitutionally protected similarly reveals a prohibition on heterosexual, as well as homosexual, sodomy.

Because the Georgia statute expresses the traditional view that sodomy is an immoral kind of conduct regardless of the identity of the persons who engage in it, I believe that a proper analysis of its constitutionality requires consideration of two questions: First, may a State totally prohibit the described conduct by means of a neutral law applying without exception to all persons subject to its jurisdiction? If not, may the State save the statute by announcing that it will only enforce the law against homosexuals? The two questions merit separate discussion.

. . . . First, the fact that the governing majority in a State has traditionally viewed a particular practice as immoral is not a sufficient reason for upholding a law prohibiting the practice; neither history nor tradition could save a law prohibiting miscegenation from constitutional attack. Second, individual decisions by married persons, concerning the intimacies of their physical relationship, even when not intended to produce offspring, are a form of "liberty" protected by the Due Process Clause of the

Fourteenth Amendment.   Moreover, this protection
extends to intimate choices by unmarried as well as
married persons.

In consideration of claims of this kind, the Court has
emphasized the individual interest in privacy, but its
decisions have actually been animated by an even more
fundamental concern. As I wrote some years ago:

> "These cases do not deal with the individual's
> interest in protection from unwarranted public
> attention, comment, or exploitation. They deal,
> rather, with the individual's right to make certain
> unusually important decisions that will affect his
> own, or his family's, destiny. The Court has
> referred to such decisions as implicating 'basic
> values,' as being 'fundamental,' and as being
> dignified by history and tradition. . . ."

Society has every right to encourage its individual
members to follow particular traditions in expressing
affection for one another and in gratifying their personal
desires. It, of course, may prohibit an individual from
imposing his will on another to satisfy his own selfish
interests.   It also may prevent an individual from
interfering with, or violating, a legally sanctioned and
protected relationship, such as marriage.   And it may
explain the relative advantages and disadvantages of
different forms of intimate expression.   But when
individual married couples are isolated from observation
by others, the way in which they voluntarily choose to
conduct their intimate relations is a matter for them - not
the State - to decide. The essential "liberty" that animated
the development of the law in cases like *Griswold*,
Eisenstadt, and *Carey* surely embraces the right to engage

in nonreproductive, sexual conduct that others may consider offensive or immoral.

Paradoxical as it may seem, our prior cases thus establish that a State may not prohibit sodomy within "the sacred precincts of marital bedrooms," or, indeed, between unmarried heterosexual adults. In all events, it is perfectly clear that the State of Georgia may not totally prohibit the conduct proscribed by . . . the Georgia Criminal Code.

If the Georgia statute cannot be enforced as it is written - if the conduct it seeks to prohibit is a protected form of liberty for the vast majority of Georgia's citizens - the State must assume the burden of justifying a selective application of its law. Either the persons to whom Georgia seeks to apply its statute do not have the same interest in "liberty" that others have, or there must be a reason why the State may be permitted to apply a generally applicable law to certain persons that it does not apply to others.

The first possibility is plainly unacceptable. Although the meaning of the principle that "all men are created equal" is not always clear, it surely must mean that every free citizen has the same interest in "liberty" that the members of the majority share. From the standpoint of the individual, the homosexual and the heterosexual have the same interest in deciding how he will live his own life, and, more narrowly, how he will conduct himself in his personal and voluntary associations with his companions. State intrusion into the private conduct of either is equally burdensome.

The second possibility is similarly unacceptable. A policy of selective application must be supported by a neutral and legitimate interest - something more substantial than a habitual dislike for, or ignorance about, the disfavored group. Neither the State nor the Court has identified any such interest in this case. The Court has posited as a justification for the Georgia statute "the presumed belief of a majority of the electorate in Georgia that homosexual sodomy is immoral and unacceptable." But the Georgia electorate has expressed no such belief - instead, its representatives enacted a law that presumably reflects the belief that *all sodomy* is immoral and unacceptable. Unless the Court is prepared to conclude that such a law is constitutional, it may not rely on the work product of the Georgia Legislature to support its holding. For the Georgia statute does not single out homosexuals as a separate class meriting special disfavored treatment.

Nor, indeed, does the Georgia prosecutor even believe that all homosexuals who violate this statute should be punished. This conclusion is evident from the fact that [Hardwick] has formally acknowledged in his complaint and in court that he has engaged, and intends to continue to engage, in the prohibited conduct, yet the State has elected not to process criminal charges against him. . . . Georgia's prohibition on private, consensual sodomy has not been enforced for decades. The record of nonenforcement, in this case and in the last several decades, belies the Attorney General's representations about the importance of the State's selective application of its generally applicable law.

Both the Georgia statute and the Georgia prosecutor thus completely fail to provide the Court with any support for the conclusion that homosexual sodomy . . . is considered unacceptable conduct in that State, and that the burden of justifying a selective application of the generally applicable law has been met.

The Court orders the dismissal of [Hardwick]'s complaint even though the State's statute prohibits all sodomy; even though that prohibition is concededly unconstitutional with respect to heterosexuals; and even though the State's ... explanations for selective application are belied by the State's own actions. . . .

I respectfully dissent.

OFFENSIVE SPEECH

HUSTLER v. FALWELL

The inside front cover of the November 1983 issue of *Hustler Magazine* featured a parody of a liquor advertisement that contained the name and picture of nationally known minister, and Moral Majority founder, Reverend Jerry Falwell. In an alleged "interview" with Falwell, entitled "Jerry Falwell Talks About His First Time," the ad parody stated Falwell's "first time" was during a drunken incestuous rendezvous with his mother in an outhouse. The ad parody went on to suggest that Falwell was a hypocrite who preached only when drunk. In small print at the bottom of the page was the disclaimer, "ad parody - not to be taken seriously."

Reverend Falwell took the ad parody very seriously and brought an action against *Hustler Magazine* and its publisher, Larry Flynt, to recover damages for invasion of privacy, libel, and the intentional infliction of emotional distress.

A federal district trial judge directed a verdict for *Hustler*/Flynt on the invasion of privacy charge and submitted the other charges to a jury. The jury found against Falwell on the defamation charge and against *Hustler*/Flynt on the intentional infliction of emotional distress charge and they awarded damages. *Hustler*/Flynt appealed to the United States Court of Appeals which affirmed the judgment of the trial court. An appeal was taken to the United States Supreme Court, which agreed to review the case in March 1987. Oral arguments were heard in December 1987 and the decision of the Court was announced in February 1988.

The opinion of the Court was delivered by Chief Justice William Rehnquist.

The complete text of *Hustler v. Falwell* can be found in volume 485 of *United States Reports.*

HUSTLER v. FALWELL

FEBRUARY 24, 1988

CHIEF JUSTICE WILLIAM REHNQUIST: Petitioner [Hustler Magazine] is a magazine of nation-wide circulation. Respondent [Jerry Falwell], a nationally known minister who has been active as a commentator on politics and public affairs, sued [Hustler and its publisher,] Larry Flynt, to recover damages for invasion of privacy, libel, and intentional infliction of emotional distress. The District Court directed a verdict against [Falwell] on the privacy claim, and submitted the other two claims to a jury. The jury found for [Hustler/Flynt] on the defamation claim, but found for [Falwell] on the claim for intentional infliction of emotional distress and awarded damages. We now consider whether this award is consistent with the First and Fourteenth Amendments of the United States Constitution.

The inside front cover of the November 1983 issue of Hustler Magazine featured a "parody" of an advertisement for Campari Liqueur that contained the name and picture of [Falwell] and was entitled "Jerry Falwell talks about his first time." This parody was modeled after actual Campari ads that included interviews with various celebrities about their "first times." Although it was apparent by the end of each interview that this meant the first time they sampled Campari, the ads clearly played on the sexual double entendre of the general subject of "first times." Copying the form and layout of these Campari ads, Hustler's editors chose [Falwell] as the featured celebrity and drafted an alleged "interview" with him in which he states that his "first time" was during a drunken

incestuous rendezvous with his mother in an outhouse.
The Hustler parody portrays [Falwell] and his mother as
drunk and immoral, and suggests that [Falwell] is a
hypocrite who preaches only when he is drunk. In small
print at the bottom of the page, the ad contains the
disclaimer, "ad parody - not to be taken seriously." The
magazine's table of contents also lists the ad as "Fiction;
Ad and Personality Parody."

Soon after the November issue of Hustler became
available to the public, [Falwell] brought [suit] in the
United States District Court for the Western District of
Virginia against Hustler Magazine, Inc., Larry C. Flynt,
and Flynt Distributing Co. [Falwell] stated in his
complaint that publication of the ad parody in Hustler
entitled him to recover damages for libel, invasion of
privacy, and intentional infliction of emotional distress.
The case proceeded to trial. At the close of the evidence,
the District Court granted a directed verdict for
[Hustler/Flynt] on the invasion of privacy claim. The
jury then found against [Falwell] on the libel claim,
specifically finding that the ad parody could not
"reasonably be understood as describing actual facts about
[Falwell] or actual events in which [he] participated."
The jury ruled for [Falwell] on the intentional infliction
of emotional distress claim, however, and stated that he
should be awarded $100,000 in compensatory damages, as
well as $50,000 each in punitive damages from
[Hustler/Flynt]. . . .

On appeal, the United States Court of Appeals for the
Fourth Circuit affirmed [upheld] the judgment against
[Hustler/Flynt]. The court rejected [their] argument that
the "actual malice" standard of *New York Times Co. v.
Sullivan* must be met before [Falwell] can recover for

emotional distress. The court agreed that because [Falwell] is concededly a public figure, [Hustler/Flynt] are "entitled to the same level of first amendment protection in the claim for intentional infliction of emotional distress that they received in [Falwell's] claim for libel." But this does not mean that a literal application of the actual malice rule is appropriate in the context of an emotional distress claim. In the court's view, the *New York Times* decision emphasized the constitutional importance not of the falsity of the statement or the defendant's disregard for the truth, but of the heightened level of culpability embodied in the requirement of "knowing . . . or reckless" conduct. Here, the *New York Times* standard is satisfied by the state-law requirement, and the jury's finding, that the defendants have acted intentionally or recklessly. The Court of Appeals then went on to reject the contention that because the jury found that the ad parody did not describe actual facts about [Falwell], the ad was an opinion that is protected by the First Amendment. As the court put it, this was "irrelevant," as the issue is "whether [the ad's] publication was sufficiently outrageous to constitute intentional infliction of emotional distress." [Hustler/Flynt] then filed a petition for rehearing [by the Court of Appeals], but this was denied by a divided court. Given the importance of the constitutional issues involved, we granted certiorari [agreed to review of the decision].

This case presents us with a novel question involving First Amendment limitations upon a State's authority to protect its citizens from the intentional infliction of emotional distress. We must decide whether a public figure may recover damages for emotional harm caused by the publication of an ad parody offensive to him, and doubtless gross and repugnant in the eyes of most.

[Falwell] would have us find that a State's interest in
protecting public figures from emotional distress is
sufficient to deny First Amendment protection to speech
that is patently offensive and is intended to inflict
emotional injury, even when that speech could not
reasonably have been interpreted as stating actual facts
about the public figure involved. This we decline to do.

At the heart of the First Amendment is the recognition of
the fundamental importance of the free flow of ideas and
opinions on matters of public interest and concern.
"[T]he freedom to speak one's mind is not only an aspect
of individual liberty - and thus a good unto itself - but
also is essential to the common quest for truth and the
vitality of society as a whole." We have therefore been
particularly vigilant to ensure that individual expressions
of ideas remain free from governmentally imposed
sanctions. The First Amendment recognizes no such thing
as a "false" idea. As Justice Holmes wrote, "[W]hen men
have realized that time has upset many fighting faiths,
they may come to believe even more than they believe the
very foundations of their own conduct that the ultimate
good desired is better reached by free trade in ideas - that
the best test of truth is the power of the thought to get
itself accepted in the competition of the market. . . ."

The sort of robust political debate encouraged by the First
Amendment is bound to produce speech that is critical of
those who hold public office or those public figures who
are "intimately involved in the resolution of important
public questions or, by reason of their fame, shape events
in areas of concern to society at large."   Justice
Frankfurter put it succinctly in *Baumgartner v. United
States*, when he said that "[o]ne of the prerogatives of
American citizenship is the right to criticize public men

and measures." Such criticism, inevitably, will not always be reasoned or moderate; public figures as well as public officials will be subject to "vehement, caustic, and sometimes unpleasantly sharp attacks." "[T]he candidate who vaunts his spotless record and sterling integrity cannot convincingly cry 'Foul!' when an opponent or an industrious reporter attempts to demonstrate the contrary."

Of course, this does not mean that *any* speech about a public figure is immune from sanction in the form of damages. Since *New York Times Co. v. Sullivan*, we have consistently ruled that a public figure may hold a speaker liable for the damage to reputation caused by publication of a defamatory falsehood, but only if the statement was made "with knowledge that it was false or with reckless disregard of whether it was false or not." False statements of fact are particularly valueless; they interfere with the truth-seeking function of the marketplace of ideas, and they cause damage to an individual's reputation that cannot easily be repaired by counterspeech, however persuasive or effective. But even though falsehoods have little value in and of themselves, they are "nevertheless inevitable in free debate," and a rule that would impose strict liability on a publisher for false factual assertions would have an undoubted "chilling" effect on speech relating to public figures that does have constitutional value. "Freedoms of expression require 'breathing space.'" This breathing space is provided by a constitutional rule that allows public figures to recover for libel or defamation only when they can prove *both* that the statement was false and that the statement was made with the requisite level of [blameworthiness].

[Falwell] argues, however, that a different standard should apply in this case because here the State seeks to prevent not reputational damage, but the severe emotional distress suffered by the person who is the subject of an offensive publication. In [Falwell]'s view, and in the view of the Court of Appeals, so long as the utterance was intended to inflict emotional distress, was outrageous, and did in fact inflict serious emotional distress, it is of no constitutional import whether the statement was a fact or an opinion, or whether it was true or false. . . . [T]he State's interest in preventing emotional harm simply outweighs whatever interest a speaker may have in speech of this type.

Generally speaking the law does not regard the intent to inflict emotional distress as one which should receive much solicitude, and it is quite understandable that most if not all jurisdictions have chosen to make it civilly culpable where the conduct in question is sufficiently "outrageous." But in the world of debate about public affairs, many things done with motives that are less than admirable are protected by the First Amendment. In *Garrison v. Louisiana*, we held that even when a speaker or writer is motivated by hatred or ill-will his expression was protected by the First Amendment:

> "Debate on public issues will not be uninhibited if the speaker must run the risk that it will be proved in court that he spoke out of hatred; even if he did speak out of hatred, utterances honestly believed contribute to the free interchange of ideas and the ascertainment of truth."

Thus while such a bad motive may be deemed controlling for purposes of . . . liability in other areas of the law, we think the First Amendment prohibits such a result in the area of public debate about public figures.

Were we to hold otherwise, there can be little doubt that political cartoonists and satirists would be subjected to damages awards without any showing that their work falsely defamed its subject. Webster's defines a caricature as "the deliberately distorted picturing or imitating of a person, literary style, etc. by exaggerating features or mannerisms for satirical effect." The appeal of the political cartoon or caricature is often based on exploration of unfortunate physical traits or politically embarrassing events - an exploration often calculated to injure the feelings of the subject of the portrayal. The art of the cartoonist is often not reasoned or evenhanded, but slashing and one-sided. One cartoonist expressed the nature of the art in these words:

> "The political cartoon is a weapon of attack, of scorn and ridicule and satire; it is least effective when it tries to pat some politician on the back. It is usually as welcome as a bee sting and is always controversial in some quarters."

Several famous examples of this type of intentionally injurious speech were drawn by Thomas Nast, probably the greatest American cartoonist to date, who was associated for many years during the post-Civil War era with Harper's Weekly. In the pages of that publication Nast conducted a graphic vendetta against William M. "Boss" Tweed and his corrupt associates in New York City's "Tweed Ring." It has been described by one historian of the subject as "a sustained attack which in its passion and effectiveness stands alone in the history of American graphic art." Another writer explains that the success of the Nast cartoon was achieved "because of the emotional impact of its presentation. It continuously goes beyond the bounds of good taste and conventional manners."

Despite their sometimes caustic nature, from the early cartoon portraying George Washington as an ass down to the present day, graphic depictions and satirical cartoons have played a prominent role in public and political debate. Nast's castigation of the Tweed Ring, Walt McDougall's characterization of presidential candidate James G. Blaine's banquet with the millionaires at Delmonico's as "The Royal Feast of Belshazzar," and numerous other efforts have undoubtedly had an effect on the course and outcome of contemporaneous debate. Lincoln's tall, gangling posture, Teddy Roosevelt's glasses and teeth, and Franklin D. Roosevelt's jutting jaw and cigarette holder have been memorialized by political cartoons with an effect that could not have been obtained by the photographer or the portrait artist. From the viewpoint of history it is clear that our political discourse would have been considerably poorer without them.

[Falwell] contends, however, that the caricature in question here was so "outrageous" as to distinguish it from more traditional political cartoons. There is no doubt that the caricature of [Falwell] and his mother published in Hustler is at best a distant cousin of the political cartoons described above, and a rather poor relation at that. If it were possible by laying down a principled standard to separate the one from the other, public discourse would probably suffer little or no harm. But we doubt that there is any such standard, and we are quite sure that the pejorative description "outrageous" does not supply one. "Outrageousness" in the area of political and social discourse has an inherent subjectiveness about it which would allow a jury to impose liability on the basis of the jurors' tastes or views, or perhaps on the basis of their dislike of a particular expression. An "outrageousness" standard thus runs afoul of our longstanding refusal to allow damages to be awarded because the speech in question may have an adverse emotional impact on the audience.   And, as we stated in *FCC v. Pacifica Foundation*:

> "[T]he fact that society may find speech offensive is not a sufficient reason for suppressing it. Indeed, if it is the speaker's opinion that gives offense, that consequence is a reason for according it constitutional protection. For it is a central tenet of the First Amendment that the government must remain neutral in the marketplace of ideas."

Admittedly, these oft-repeated First Amendment principles, like other principles, are subject to limitations. We recognized in *Pacifica Foundation*, that speech that is "'vulgar,' 'offensive,' and 'shocking'" is "not entitled to absolute   constitutional   protection   under   all circumstances." In *Chaplinsky v. New Hampshire*, we held that a state could lawfully punish an individual for the use of insulting "'fighting' words - those which by their very utterance inflict injury or tend to incite an immediate breach of the peace." These limitations are but recognition of the observation in *Dun & Bradstreet v. Greenmoss Builders* that this Court has "long recognized that not all speech is of equal First Amendment importance." But the sort of expression involved in this case does not seem to us to be governed by any exception to the general First Amendment principles stated above.

We conclude that public figures and public officials may not recover for the . . . intentional infliction of emotional distress by reason of publications such as the one here at issue without showing in ,addition that the publication contains a false statement of fact which was made with "actual malice," *i.e.*, with knowledge that the statement was false or with reckless disregard as to whether or not it was true. This is not merely a "blind application" of the *New York Times* standard, it reflects our considered judgment that such a standard is necessary to give adequate "breathing space" to the freedoms protected by the First Amendment.

Here it is clear that [Jerry] Falwell is a "public figure" for purposes of First Amendment law. The jury found against [Falwell] on his libel claim when it decided that the Hustler ad parody could not "reasonably be understood as describing actual facts about [Falwell] or actual events in which [he] participated." The Court of Appeals interpreted the jury's finding to be that the ad parody "was not reasonably believable," and in accordance with our custom we accept this finding. [Falwell] is thus relegated to his claim for damages awarded by the jury for the intentional infliction of emotional distress by "outrageous" conduct. But for [the] reasons heretofore stated this claim cannot, consistently with the First Amendment, form a basis for the award of damages when the conduct in question is the publication of a caricature such as the ad parody involved here. The judgment of the Court of Appeals is accordingly *Reversed.*

THE RIGHT TO DIE

CRUZAN v. MISSOURI

IN THE MATTER OF
KAREN ANN QUINLAN

The Right To Die Case begins in Missouri on January 11, 1983. That night, 25-year-old Nancy Beth Cruzan suffered massive neurological injuries in an automobile accident that left her irreversibly brain-damaged.

Ten months after the accident, her parents, Lester and Joyce Cruzan, appointed by a local court as her co-guardians, asked that a surgically-implanted feeding tube, which was keeping their daughter alive, be removed and that Nancy be allowed to die. The state hospital refused to do so without a Court's permission. The parents of Nancy Beth Cruzan sued, on her behalf, the Missouri State Department of Health to end their "death prolonging procedures."

The trial court found for the Cruzans, stating that Nancy, who had once told a friend she would not want to live if she could not live a normal life, had a fundamental right under the State and Federal Constitutions to, through her parents, refuse artificial life-sustaining measures. The Department of Health appealed the decision to the Missouri Supreme Court, which reversed the trial court decision, stating that no such Constitutional rights existed and that "no person can assume the choice for an incompetent" in matters of life and death without convincing and reliable evidence.

The U.S. Supreme Court agreed to review the Missouri Supreme Court's decision on July 3, 1989. Oral arguments were heard on December 6, 1989 and a decision given on June 25, 1990.

The 5-4 decision of the Court was given by Chief Justice Rehnquist.

The complete text of *Cruzan v. Missouri* appears in volume 497 of *United States Reports.*

CRUZAN v. MISSOURI

JUNE 25, 1990

CHIEF JUSTICE WILLIAM REHNQUIST: Petitioner Nancy Beth Cruzan was rendered incompetent as a result of severe injuries sustained during an automobile accident. Copetitioners Lester and Joyce Cruzan, Nancy's parents and co-guardians, sought a court order directing the withdrawal of their daughter's artificial feeding and hydration equipment after it became apparent that she had virtually no chance of recovering her cognitive faculties. The Supreme Court of Missouri held that because there was no clear and convincing evidence of Nancy's desire to have life-sustaining treatment withdrawn under such circumstances, her parents lacked authority to effectuate such a request. We granted certiorari [agreed to review the case], and now affirm [uphold].

On the night of January 11, 1983, Nancy Cruzan lost control of her car as she traveled down Elm Road in Jasper County, Missouri. The vehicle overturned, and Cruzan was discovered lying face down in a ditch without detectable respiratory or cardiac function. Paramedics were able to restore her breathing and heartbeat at the accident site, and she was transported to a hospital in an unconscious state. An attending neurosurgeon diagnosed her as having sustained probable cerebral contusions compounded by significant anoxia (lack of oxygen). The Missouri trial court in this case found that permanent brain damage generally results after 6 minutes in an anoxic state; it was estimated that Cruzan was deprived of oxygen from 12 to 14 minutes. She remained in a coma

for approximately three weeks and then progressed to an
unconscious state in which she was able to orally ingest
some nutrition. In order to ease feeding and further the
recovery, surgeons implanted a gastrostomy feeding and
hydration tube in Cruzan with the consent of her then
husband.   Subsequent   rehabilitative   efforts   proved
unavailing. She now lies in a Missouri state hospital in
what is commonly referred to as a persistent vegetative
state: generally, a condition in which a person exhibits
motor reflexes but evinces no indications of significant
cognitive function. The State of Missouri is bearing the
cost of her care.

After it had become apparent that Nancy Cruzan had
virtually no chance of regaining her mental faculties her
parents asked hospital employees to terminate the
artificial nutrition and hydration procedures. All agree
that such a removal would cause her death.   The
employees refused to honor the request without court
approval.   The   parents then sought and received
authorization from the state trial court for termination.
The court found that a person in Nancy's condition had a
fundamental right under the State and Federal
Constitutions to refuse or direct the withdrawal of "death
prolonging procedures."   The court also found that
Nancy's "expressed thoughts at age twenty-five in
somewhat serious conversation with a housemate friend
that if sick or injured she would not wish to continue her
life unless she could live at least halfway normally
suggests that given her present condition she would not
wish to continue on with her nutrition and hydration."

The Supreme Court of Missouri reversed by a divided
vote. The court recognized a right to refuse treatment
embodied in the common-law doctrine of informed

consent, but expressed skepticism about the application of that doctrine in the circumstances of this case. The court also declined to read a broad right of privacy into the State Constitution which would "support the right of a person to refuse medical treatment in every circumstance," and expressed doubt as to whether such a right existed under the United States Constitution. It then decided that the Missouri Living Will statute embodied a state policy strongly favoring the preservation of life. The court found that Cruzan's statements to her roommate regarding her desire to live or die under certain conditions were "unreliable for the purpose of determining her intent, and thus insufficient to support the co-guardians claim to exercise substituted judgment on Nancy's behalf." It rejected the argument that Cruzan's parents were entitled to order the termination of her medical treatment, concluding that "no person can assume that choice for an incompetent in the absence of the formalities required under Missouri's Living Will statutes or the clear and convincing, inherently reliable evidence absent here." The court also expressed its view that "[b]road policy questions bearing on life and death are more properly addressed by representative assemblies" than judicial bodies.

We [agreed] to consider the question of whether Cruzan has a right under the United States Constitution which would require the hospital to withdraw life-sustaining treatment from her under these circumstances.

At common law, even the touching of one person by another without consent and without legal justification was a battery. Before the turn of the century, this Court observed that "[n]o right is held more sacred, or is more carefully guarded, by the common law, than the right of every individual to the possession and control of his own person, free from all restraint or interference of others, unless by clear and unquestionable authority of law." This notion of bodily integrity has been embodied in the requirement that informed consent is generally required for medical treatment. Justice Cardozo, while on the Court of Appeals of New York, aptly described this doctrine: "Every human being of adult years and sound mind has a right to determine what shall be done with his own body; and a surgeon who performs an operation without his patient's consent commits an assault, for which he is liable in damages." The informed consent doctrine has become firmly entrenched in American . . . law.

The logical corollary of the doctrine of informed consent is that the patient generally possesses the right not to consent, that is, to refuse treatment. Until about 15 years ago . . . the number of right-to-refuse-treatment decisions were relatively few. Most of the earlier cases involved patients who refused medical treatment forbidden by their religious beliefs, thus implicating First Amendment rights as well as common law rights of self-determination. More recently, however, with the advance of medical technology capable of sustaining life well past the point where natural forces would have brought certain death in earlier times, cases involving the right to refuse life-sustaining treatment have burgeoned.

In the *Quinlan* case, young Karen Quinlan suffered severe brain damage as the result of anoxia, and entered a persistent vegetative state. Karen's father sought judicial approval to disconnect his daughter's respirator. The New Jersey Supreme Court granted the relief, holding that Karen had a right of privacy grounded in the Federal

Constitution to terminate treatment. Recognizing that this right was not absolute, however, the court balanced it against asserted state interests. Noting that the State's interest "weakens and the individual's right to privacy grows as the degree of bodily invasion increases and the prognosis dims," the court concluded that the state interests had to give way in that case. The court also concluded that the "only practical way" to prevent the loss of Karen's privacy right due to her incompetence was to allow her guardian and family to decide "whether she would exercise it in these circumstances."

After *Quinlan*, however, most courts have based a right to refuse treatment either solely on the common law right to informed consent or on both the common law right and a constitutional privacy right. . . .

Many of the later cases build on the principles established in *Quinlan*, *Saikewicz* and *Storar/Eichner*. For instance, in *In re Conroy*, the same court that decided *Quinlan* considered whether a nasogastric feeding tube could be removed from an 84-year-old incompetent nursing-home resident suffering irreversible mental and physical ailments. While recognizing that a federal right of privacy might apply in the case, the court, contrary to its approach in *Quinlan*, decided to base its decision on the common-law right to self-determination and informed consent. "On balance, the right to self-determination ordinarily outweighs any countervailing state interests, and competent persons generally are permitted to refuse medical treatment, even at the risk of death. Most of the cases that have held otherwise, unless they involved the interest in protecting innocent third parties, have concerned the patient's competency to make a rational and considered choice."

Reasoning that the right of self-determination should not
be lost merely because an individual is unable to sense a
violation of it, the court held that incompetent individuals
retain a right to refuse treatment. It also held that such a
right could be exercised by a surrogate decisionmaker
using a "subjective" standard when there was clear
evidence that the incompetent person would have
exercised it. Where such evidence was lacking, the court
held that an individual's right could still be invoked in
certain circumstances under objective "best interest"
standards. Thus, if some trustworthy evidence existed
that the individual would have wanted to terminate
treatment, but not enough to clearly establish a person's
wishes for purposes of the subjective standard, and the
burden of a prolonged life from the experience of pain
and suffering markedly outweighed its satisfactions,
treatment could be terminated under a "limited-objective"
standard. Where no trustworthy evidence existed, and a
person's suffering would make the administration of life-
sustaining treatment inhumane, a "pure-objective"
standard could be used to terminate treatment. If none of
these conditions obtained, the court held it was best to err
in favor of preserving life.

The court also rejected certain categorical distinctions that
had been drawn in prior refusal-of-treatment cases as
lacking substance for decision purposes: the distinction
between actively hastening death by terminating
treatment and passively allowing a person to die of a
disease; between treating individuals as an initial matter
versus withdrawing treatment afterwards; between
ordinary versus extraordinary treatment; and between
treatment by artificial feeding versus other forms of life-
sustaining medical procedures. As to the last item, the
court acknowledged the "emotional significance" of food,

but noted that feeding by implanted tubes is a "medical procedur[e] with inherent risks and possible side effects, instituted by skilled health-care providers to compensate for impaired physical functioning" which analytically was equivalent to artificial breathing using a respirator.

In contrast to *Conroy*, the Court of Appeals of New York recently refused to accept less than the clearly expressed wishes of a patient before permitting the exercise of her right to refuse treatment by a surrogate decisionmaker. There, the court, over the objection of the patient's family members, granted an order to insert a feeding tube into a 77-year-old woman rendered incompetent as a result of several strokes. While continuing to recognize a common-law right to refuse treatment, the court rejected the substituted judgment approach for asserting it "because it is inconsistent with our fundamental commitment to the notion that no person or court should substitute its judgment as to what would be an acceptable quality of life for another. Consequently, we adhere to the view that, despite its pitfalls and inevitable uncertainties, the inquiry must always be narrowed to the patient's expressed intent, with every effort made to minimize the opportunity for error." The court held that the record lacked the requisite clear and convincing evidence of the patient's expressed intent to withhold life-sustaining treatment.

Other courts have found state statutory law relevant to the resolution of these issues. In *Conservatorship of Drabick*, the California Court of Appeal authorized the removal of a nasogastric feeding tube from a 44-year-old man who was in a persistent vegetative state as a result of an auto accident. ... [T]he court held that a state probate statute authorized the patient's conservator to order the withdrawal of life-sustaining treatment when such a decision was made in good faith based on medical advice and the conservatee's best interests. . . .

In *In re Estate of Longeway*, the Supreme Court of Illinois considered whether a 76-year-old woman rendered incompetent from a series of strokes had a right to the discontinuance of artificial nutrition and hydration. Noting that the boundaries of a federal right of privacy were uncertain, the court found a right to refuse treatment in the doctrine of informed consent. The court further held that the State Probate Act impliedly authorized a guardian to exercise a ward's right to refuse artificial sustenance in the event that the ward was terminally ill and irreversibly comatose. . . .

As these cases demonstrate, the common-law doctrine of informed consent is viewed as generally encompassing the right of a competent individual to refuse medical treatment. Beyond that, these decisions demonstrate both similarity and diversity in their approach to decision of what all agree is a perplexing question with unusually strong moral and ethical overtones. State courts have available to them for decision a number of sources - state constitutions, statutes, and common law - which are not available to us. In this Court, the question is simply and starkly whether the United States Constitution prohibits Missouri from choosing the rule of decision which it did. This is the first case in which we have been squarely presented with the issue of whether the United States Constitution grants what is in common parlance referred to as a "right to die." We follow the judicious counsel of our decision in *Twin City Bank v. Nebeker*, where we said that in deciding "a question of such magnitude and importance . . . it is the [better] part of wisdom not to attempt, by any general statement, to cover every possible phase of the subject."

The Fourteenth Amendment provides that no State shall "deprive any person of life, liberty, or property, without due process of law." The principle that a competent person has a constitutionally protected liberty interest in refusing unwanted medical treatment may be inferred from our prior decisions. In *Jacobson v. Massachusetts*, for instance, the Court balanced an individual's liberty interest in declining an unwanted smallpox vaccine against the State's interest in preventing disease. Decisions prior to the incorporation of the Fourth Amendment into the Fourteenth Amendment analyzed searches and seizures involving the body under the Due Process Clause and were thought to implicate substantial liberty interests.

Just this Term, in the course of holding that a State's procedures for administering antipsychotic medication to prisoners were sufficient to satisfy due process concerns, we recognized that prisoners possess "a significant liberty interest in avoiding the unwanted administration of antipsychotic drugs under the Due Process Clause of the Fourteenth Amendment." ...

But determining that a person has a "liberty interest" under the Due Process Clause does not end the inquiry; "whether respondent's constitutional rights have been violated must be determined by balancing his liberty interests against the relevant state interests."

[Cruzan's guardians] insist that . . . the forced administration of life-sustaining medical treatment, and even of artificially-delivered food and water essential to life, would implicate a competent person's liberty interest. Although we think the logic of the cases discussed above would embrace such a liberty interest, the dramatic consequences involved in refusal of such treatment would [answer the question of] whether the deprivation of that interest is constitutionally permissible. But for purposes of this case, we assume that the United States Constitution would grant a competent person a constitutionally protected right to refuse lifesaving hydration and nutrition.

[Cruzan's guardians] go on to assert that an incompetent person should possess the same right in this respect as is possessed by a competent person. They rely primarily on our decisions in *Parham v. J.R.*, and *Youngberg v. Romeo.* In *Parham*, we held that a mentally disturbed minor child had a liberty interest in "not being confined unnecessarily for medical treatment," but we certainly did not intimate that such a minor child, after commitment, would have a liberty interest in refusing treatment. In *Youngberg*, we held that a seriously retarded adult had a liberty interest in safety and freedom from bodily restraint. *Youngberg*, however, did not deal with decisions to administer or withhold medical treatment.

The difficulty with [Cruzan's guardians'] claim is that in a sense it begs the question: an incompetent person is not able to make an informed and voluntary choice to exercise a hypothetical right to refuse treatment or any other right. Such a "right" must be exercised for her, if at all, by some sort of surrogate. Here, Missouri has in effect recognized that under certain circumstances a surrogate may act for the patient in electing to have hydration and nutrition withdrawn in such a way as to cause death, but it has established a procedural safeguard to assure that the action of the surrogate conforms as best it may to the wishes expressed by the patient while competent. Missouri requires that evidence of the incompetent's wishes as to the withdrawal of treatment be proved by clear and convincing evidence. The question, then, is whether the United States Constitution forbids the establishment of this procedural requirement by the State. We hold that it does not.

Whether or not Missouri's clear and convincing evidence requirement comports with the United States Constitution depends in part on what interests the State may properly seek to protect in this situation. Missouri relies on its interest in the protection and preservation of human life, and there can be no gainsaying this interest. As a general matter, the States - indeed, all civilized nations - demonstrate their commitment to life by treating homicide as serious crime. Moreover, the majority of States in this country have laws imposing criminal penalties on one who assists another to commit suicide. We do not think a State is required to remain neutral in the face of an informed and voluntary decision by a physically-able adult to starve to death.

But in the context presented here, a State has more particular interests at stake. The choice between life and death is a deeply personal decision of obvious and overwhelming finality. We believe Missouri may legitimately seek to safeguard the personal element of this choice through the imposition of heightened evidentiary requirements. It cannot be disputed that the Due Process Clause protects an interest in life as well as an interest in refusing life-sustaining medical treatment. Not all incompetent patients will have loved ones available to serve as surrogate decisionmakers. And even where

family members are present, "[t]here will, of course, be
some unfortunate situations in which family members will
not act to protect a patient." A State is entitled to guard
against potential abuses in such situations. Similarly, a
State is entitled to consider that a judicial proceeding to
make a determination regarding an incompetent's wishes
may very well not be an adversarial one, with the added
guarantee of accurate factfinding that the adversary
process brings with it. Finally, we think a State may
properly decline to make judgments about the "quality" of
life that a particular individual may enjoy, and simply
assert an unqualified interest in the preservation of
human life to be weighed against the constitutionally
protected interests of the individual.

In our view, Missouri has permissibly sought to advance
these interests through the adoption of a "clear and
convincing" standard of proof to govern such proceedings.
"The function of a standard of proof, as that concept is
embodied in the Due Process Clause and in the realm of
factfinding, is to 'instruct the factfinder concerning the
degree of confidence our society thinks he should have in
the correctness of factual conclusions for a particular type
of adjudication.'"   "This Court has mandated an
intermediate standard of proof - 'clear and convincing
evidence' - when the individual interests at stake in a state
proceeding are both 'particularly important' and 'more
substantial than mere loss of money.'"   Thus, such a
standard has been required in deportation proceedings, in
denaturalization proceedings, in civil commitment
proceedings, and in proceedings for the termination of
parental rights. Further, this level of proof, "or an even
higher one, has traditionally been imposed in cases
involving allegations of civil fraud, and in a variety of

other kinds of civil cases involving such issues as . . . lost wills, oral contracts to make bequests, and the like."

We think it self-evident that the interests at stake in the [present] proceedings are more substantial, both on an individual and societal level, than those involved in [an ordinary] dispute. But not only does the standard of proof reflect the importance of a particular adjudication, it also serves as "a societal judgment about how the risk of error should be distributed between the litigants." The more stringent the burden of proof a party must bear, the more that party bears the risk of an erroneous decision. We believe that Missouri may permissibly place an increased risk of an erroneous decision on those seeking to terminate an incompetent individual's life-sustaining treatment. An erroneous decision not to terminate results in a maintenance of the status quo; the possibility of subsequent developments such as advancements in medical science, the discovery of new evidence regarding the patient's intent, changes in the law, or simply the unexpected death of the patient despite the administration of life-sustaining treatment, at least create the potential that a wrong decision will eventually be corrected or its impact mitigated. An erroneous decision to withdraw life-sustaining treatment, however, is not susceptible of correction. In *Santosky*, one of the factors which led the Court to require proof by clear and convincing evidence in a proceeding to terminate parental rights was that a decision in such a case was final and irrevocable. The same must surely be said of the decision to discontinue hydration and nutrition of a patient such as Nancy Cruzan, which all agree will result in her death.

It is also worth noting that most, if not all, States simply forbid oral testimony entirely in determining the wishes of parties in transactions which, while important, simply do not have the consequences that a decision to terminate a person's life does. At common law and by statute in most States, the parole evidence rule prevents the variations of the terms of a written contract by oral testimony. The statute of frauds makes unenforceable oral contracts to leave property by will, and statutes regulating the making of wills universally require that those instruments be in writing. There is no doubt that statutes requiring wills to be in writing, and statutes of frauds which require that a contract to make a will be in writing, on occasion frustrate the effectuation of the intent of a particular decedent, just as Missouri's requirement of proof in this case may have frustrated the effectuation of the not-fully-expressed desires of Nancy Cruzan. But the Constitution does not require general rules to work faultlessly; no general rule can.

In sum, we conclude that a State may apply a clear and convincing evidence standard in proceedings where a guardian seeks to discontinue nutrition and hydration of a person diagnosed to be in a persistent vegetative state. We note that many courts which have adopted some sort of substituted judgment procedure in situations like this, whether they limit consideration of evidence to the prior expressed wishes of the incompetent individual, or whether they allow more general proof of what the individual's decision would have been, require a clear and convincing standard of proof for such evidence.

The Supreme Court of Missouri held that in this case the testimony [offered] at trial did not amount to clear and convincing proof of the patient's desire to have hydration and nutrition withdrawn. In so doing, it reversed a decision of the Missouri trial court which had found that the evidence "suggest[ed]" Nancy Cruzan would not have desired to continue such measures, but which had not adopted the standard of "clear and convincing evidence" enunciated by the Supreme Court. The testimony [offered] at trial consisted primarily of Nancy Cruzan's statements made to a housemate about a year before her accident that she would not want to live should she face life as a "vegetable," and other observations to the same effect. The observations did not deal in terms with withdrawal of medical treatment or of hydration and nutrition. We cannot say that the Supreme Court of Missouri committed constitutional error in reaching the conclusion that it did.

[Cruzan's guardians] alternatively contend that Missouri must accept the "substituted judgment" of close family members even in the absence of substantial proof that their views reflect the views of the patient. They rely primarily upon our decisions in *Michael H. v. Gerald D.* and *Parham v. J.R.* But we do not think these cases support their claim. In *Michael H.*, we *upheld* the constitutionality of California's favored treatment of traditional family relationships; such a holding may not be turned around into a constitutional requirement that a State must recognize the primacy of those relationships in a situation like this. And in *Parham*, where the patient was a minor, we also *upheld* the constitutionality of a state scheme in which parents made certain decisions for mentally ill minors. Here again [Cruzan's guardians] would seek to turn a decision which allowed a State to rely on family decisionmaking into a constitutional requirement that the State recognize such decisionmaking. But constitutional law does not work that way.

No doubt is engendered by anything in this record but that Nancy Cruzan's mother and father are loving and caring parents. If the State were required by the United States Constitution to repose a right of "substituted judgment" with anyone, the Cruzans would surely qualify. But we do not think the Due Process Clause requires the State to repose judgment on these matters with anyone but the patient herself. Close family members may have a strong feeling - a feeling not at all ignoble or unworthy, but not entirely disinterested, either - that they do not wish to witness the continuation of the life of a loved one which they regard as hopeless, meaningless, and even degrading. But there is no automatic assurance that the view of close family members will necessarily be the same as the patient's would have been had she been confronted with the prospect of her situation while competent. All of the reasons previously discussed for allowing Missouri to require clear and convincing evidence of the patient's wishes lead us to conclude that the State may choose to defer only to those wishes, rather than confide the decision to close family members.

The judgment of the Supreme Court of Missouri is affirmed [upheld].

On December 26, 1990 - nearly 8 years after her accident, 6 months after the Supreme Court's landmark decision, and 12 days after a County judge allowed the removal of the feeding tube - Nancy Beth Cruzan, age 33, died.

Fifteen years prior to the Landmark Right To Die Decision, *Cruzan v. Missouri,* Karen Ann Quinlan, twenty-one, fell into an irreversible coma and was placed on life support in a Morris County, New Jersey hospital. Her family, a court-appointed guardian, her doctors, the hospital, the County and the State fought over the continuance or cessation of that life support. *In The Matter of Karen Quinlan* was decided by the New Jersey Supreme Court. The decision, referred to in *Cruzan,* is included here for its legal significance.

In April 1975 Karen Ann Quinlan stopped breathing - twice, each time for over 15 minutes - suffering severe brain damage. She fell into a chronic vegetative state and was placed on a respirator to assist her breathing and a feeding tube for nourishment. Her doctors concluded there was no hope of any change. Her father, Joseph Quinlan, asked a New Jersey Court to authorize the removal of his daughter from the respirator so that she could die naturally. Karen Ann Quinlan was described to the court as emaciated, having suffered a weight loss of at least 40 pounds; her posture was described as fetal-like and grotesque. The court refused.

Joseph Quinlan appealed the lower court decision, based on his daughter's First, Eighth, and Fourteenth Amendment rights, to the New Jersey Supreme Court.

The complete text of *In The Matter of Karen Ann Quinlan* can be found in volume 70 of *New Jersey Reports.*

IN THE MATTER OF KAREN ANN QUINLAN

March 31, 1976

CHIEF JUSTICE RICHARD J. HUGHES delivered the opinion of the Court: The central figure in this tragic case is Karen Ann Quinlan, a New Jersey resident. At the age of 22, she lies in a debilitated and allegedly moribund state at Saint Clare's Hospital in Denville, New Jersey. The litigation has to do, in final analysis, with her life - its continuance or cessation - and the responsibilities, rights and duties, with regard to any fateful decision concerning it, of her family, her guardian, her doctors, the hospital, the State through its law enforcement authorities, and finally the courts of justice.

. . . . [R]elying on claimed constitutional rights of free exercise of religion, of privacy and of protection against cruel and unusual punishment, Karen Quinlan's father sought judicial authority to withdraw the life-sustaining mechanisms temporarily preserving his daughter's life, and his appointment as guardian of her person to that end. His request was opposed by her doctors, the hospital, the Morris County Prosecutor, the State of New Jersey, and her guardian *ad litem* [an individual appointed by the court as the guardian of her person].

. . . . On the night of April 15, 1975, for reasons still unclear, Karen Quinlan ceased breathing for at least two 15 minute periods. She received some ineffectual mouth-to-mouth resuscitation from friends. She was taken by ambulance to Newton Memorial Hospital. There she had a temperature of 100 degrees, her pupils were unreactive and she was unresponsive even to deep pain. The history at the time of her admission to that hospital was essentially incomplete and uninformative.

Three days later, Dr. [Robert J.] Morse [a neurologist] examined Karen at the request of the Newton admitting physician, Dr. McGee. He found her comatose with evidence of decortication, a condition relating to derangement of the cortex of the brain causing a physical posture in which the upper extremities are flexed and the lower extremities are extended. She required a respirator to assist her breathing. Dr. Morse was unable to obtain an adequate account of the circumstances and events leading up to Karen's admission to the Newton Hospital. Such initial history or etiology is crucial in neurological diagnosis. Relying as he did upon the Newton Memorial records and his own examination, he concluded that prolonged lack of oxygen in the bloodstream, anoxia, was identified with her condition as he saw it upon first observation. When she was later transferred to Saint Clare's Hospital she was still unconscious, still on a respirator and a tracheotomy had been performed. On her arrival Dr. Morse conducted extensive and detailed examinations. An electroencephalogram (EEG) . . . was . . . characterized . . . as "abnormal but it showed some activity and was consistent with her clinical state." Other significant neurological tests . . . were normal in result. Dr. Morse testified that Karen has been in a state of coma, lack of consciousness, since he began treating her. He explained that there are basically two types of coma, sleep-like unresponsiveness and awake unresponsiveness. Karen was originally in a sleeplike unresponsive condition but soon developed "sleep-wake" cycles, apparently a normal improvement for comatose patients occurring within three to four weeks. In the awake cycle she blinks, cries out and does things of that sort but is still totally unaware of anyone or anything around her.

Dr. Morse and other expert physicians who examined her characterized Karen as being in a "chronic persistent vegetative state." . . .

Dr. Morse . . . believed with certainty that Karen Quinlan is not "brain dead." . . .

Because Karen's neurological condition affects her respiratory ability . . . she requires a respirator to assist her breathing. . . . Attempts to "wean" her from the respirator were unsuccessful and have been abandoned.

The experts believe that Karen cannot now survive without the assistance of the respirator; that exactly how long she would live without it is unknown; that the strong likelihood is that death would follow soon after its removal, and that removal would also risk further brain damage and would curtail the assistance the respirator presently provides in warding off infection.

It seemed to be the consensus not only of the treating physicians but also of the several qualified experts who testified in the case, that removal from the respirator would not conform to medical practices, standards and traditions.

. . . . Karen is described as emaciated, having suffered a weight loss of at least 40 pounds, and undergoing a continuing deteriorative process. Her posture is described as fetal-like and grotesque; there is extreme flexion-rigidity of the arms, legs and related muscles and her joints are severely rigid and deformed.

. . . . Severe brain and associated damage . . . has left
Karen in a chronic and persistent vegetative state. No
form of treatment which can cure or improve that
condition is known or available. As nearly as may be
determined . . . she can *never* be restored to cognitive or
sapient life. . . .

She is debilitated and moribund and although fairly stable
at the time of argument before us . . . no physician risked
the opinion that she could live more than a year and
indeed she may die much earlier. Excellent medical and
nursing care so far has been able to ward off the constant
threat of infection, to which she is peculiarly susceptible
because of the respirator, the tracheal tube and other
incidents of care in her vulnerable condition. Her life
accordingly is sustained by the respirator and tubal
feeding, and removal from the respirator would cause her
death soon, although the time cannot be stated with more
precision.

. . . . Developments in medical technology have
[confused] the use of the traditional definition of death.
Efforts have been made to define irreversible coma as a
new criterion for death. . . .

The [modern] standards, carefully delineated, included
absence of response to pain or other stimuli, pupilary . . .
corneal, pharyngeal and other reflexes, blood pressure,
spontaneous respiration, as well as "flat" . . . [EEG's] and
the like, with all tests repeated "at least 24 hours later
with no change." In such circumstances, where all of such
criteria have been met as showing "brain death," the
[Harvard Medical School Ad Hoc] Committee [which
designed these standards] recommends with regard to the
respirator:

The patient's condition can be determined only by a physician. When the patient is hopelessly damaged as defined above, the family and all colleagues who have participated in major decisions concerning the patient, and all nurses involved, should be so informed. Death is to be declared and *then* the respirator turned off. The decision to do this and the responsibility for it are to be taken by the physician-in-charge, in consultation with one or more physicians who have been directly involved in the case. It is unsound and undesirable to force the family to make the decision.

But, as indicated, it was the consensus of medical testimony in the [present] case that Karen, for all her disability, met none of these criteria, nor indeed any comparable criteria . . . representing . . . prevailing and accepted medical standards.

We have adverted to the "brain death" concept and Karen's disassociation with any of its criteria, to emphasize the basis of the medical decision made by Dr. Morse. . . . His refusal [to withdraw the life support mechanisms] was based upon his conception of medical standards, practice and ethics. . . .

We agree with the trial court that that decision was in accord with Dr. Morse's conception of medical standards and practice.

We turn to . . . the application for guardianship. . . . The character and general suitability of Joseph Quinlan as guardian for his daughter, in ordinary circumstances, could not be doubted. The record bespeaks the high

degree of familial love which pervaded the home of
Joseph Quinlan and reached out fully to embrace Karen,
although she was living elsewhere at the time of her
collapse. The proofs [facts revealed in the trial court]
showed him to be deeply religious, imbued with a
morality so sensitive that months of tortured indecision
preceded his belated conclusion (despite earlier moral
judgments reached by the other family members, but
unexpressed to him in order not to influence him) to seek
the termination of life-supportive measures sustaining
Karen. A communicant of the Roman Catholic Church, as
were other family members, he first sought solace in
private prayer looking with confidence, as he says, to the
Creator, first for the recovery of Karen and then, if that
were not possible, for guidance with respect to the
awesome decision confronting him.

To confirm the moral rightness of the decision he was
about to make he consulted with his parish priest and
later with the Catholic chaplain of Saint Clare's Hospital.
He would not, he testified, have sought termination if that
act were to be morally wrong or in conflict with the
tenets of the religion he so profoundly respects. He was
disabused of doubt, however, when the position of the
Roman Catholic Church was made known to him. . . .
While it is not usual for matters of religious dogma or
concepts to enter a civil litigation . . . they were rightly
admitted in evidence here. The judge was bound to
measure the character and motivations in all respects of
Joseph Quinlan as prospective guardian; and insofar as
these religious matters bore upon them, they were
properly scrutinized and considered by the court.

. . . . Bishop [Lawrence B.] Casey . . . validated the
decision of Joseph Quinlan:

Competent medical testimony has established that Karen Ann Quinlan has no reasonable hope of recovery from her comatose state by the use of any available medical procedures. The continuance of mechanical (cardiorespiratory) supportive measures to sustain continuation of her body functions and her life constitute extraordinary means of treatment. *Therefore, the decision of Joseph Quinlan to request the discontinuance of this treatment is, according to the teachings of the Catholic Church, a morally correct decision.*

. . . . Before turning to the legal and constitutional issues involved, we feel it essential to reiterate that the "Catholic view" . . . is considered by the Court only in the aspect of its impact upon the conscience, motivation and purpose of the intending guardian, Joseph Quinlan, and not as a precedent [rule established by prior cases] in terms of the civil law.

. . . . [T]he Court confronts and responds to three basic issues:

1. Was the trial court correct in denying the specific relief requested by [Joseph Quinlan], *i.e.,* authorization for termination of the life-supporting apparatus, on the case presented to him? Our determination on that question is in the affirmative.

2. Was the court correct in withholding letters of guardianship from [Joseph Quinlan] and appointing in his stead a stranger? On that issue our determination is in the negative.

3. Should this Court, in the light of the foregoing conclusions, grant . . . relief to [Joseph Quinlan]? On that question our Court's determination is in the affirmative.

. . . . The father of Karen Quinlan is certainly no stranger to the present controversy. His interests are real and adverse and he raises questions of surpassing importance. Manifestly, he has standing [the right] to assert his daughter's constitutional rights, she being incompetent to do so.

. . . . [T]he right to religious beliefs is absolute but conduct in pursuance thereof is not wholly immune from governmental restraint. So it is that, for the sake of life, courts sometimes (but not always) order blood transfusions for Jehovah's Witnesses (whose religious beliefs abhor such procedure), forbid exposure to death from handling virulent snakes or ingesting poison (interfering with deeply held religious sentiments in such regard), and protect the public health as in the case of compulsory vaccination (over the strongest of religious objections). The public interest is thus considered paramount, without essential dissolution of respect for religious beliefs. . . .

Similarly inapplicable to the case before us is the Constitution's Eighth Amendment protection against cruel and unusual punishment which, as held by the trial court, is not relevant to situations other than the imposition of penal sanctions. . . .

It is the issue of the constitutional right of privacy that has given us most concern, in the exceptional circumstances of this case. Here a loving parent . . . raising the rights of his incompetent and profoundly damaged daughter, probably irreversibly doomed to no more than a biologically vegetative remnant of life, is before the court. He seeks authorization to abandon specialized technological procedures which can only maintain for a time a body having no potential for resumption or continuance of other than a "vegetative" existence.

We have no doubt, in these unhappy circumstances, that if Karen were herself miraculously lucid for an interval (not altering the existing prognosis of the condition to which she would soon return) and preceptive of her irreversible condition, she could effectively decide upon discontinuance of the life-support apparatus, even if it meant the prospect of natural death. . . .

We have no hesitancy in deciding . . . that no external compelling interest of the State could compel Karen to endure the unendurable, only to vegetate a few measurable months with no realistic possibility of returning to any semblance of cognitive or sapient life. . . .

Although the Constitution does not explicitly mention a right of privacy, Supreme Court decisions have recognized that a right of personal privacy exists and that certain areas of privacy are guaranteed under the Constitution. . . .

The Court in *Griswold [v. Connecticut]* found the unwritten constitutional right of privacy to exist in the . . . Bill of Rights. . . . Presumably this right is broad enough to encompass a patient's decision to decline medical treatment under certain circumstances, in much the same way as it is broad enough to encompass a woman's decision to terminate pregnancy under certain conditions.

. . . . The claimed interests of the State in this case are essentially the preservation and sanctity of human life and defense of the right of the physician to administer medical treatment according to his best judgment. In this case the doctors say that removing Karen from the respirator will conflict with their professional judgment. The plaintiff [Joseph Quinlan] answers that Karen's present treatment serves only a maintenance function; that the respirator cannot cure or improve her condition but at best can only prolong her inevitable slow deterioration and death; and that the interests of the patient, as seen by her surrogate, the guardian, must be evaluated by the court as predominant, even in the face of an opinion *contra* [against] by the present attending physicians. [Joseph Quinlan]'s distinction is significant. . . . We think that the State's interest *[against]* weakens and the individual's right to privacy grows as the degree of bodily invasion increases and the prognosis dims. Ultimately there comes a point at which the individual's rights overcome the State interest. It is for that reason that we believe Karen's choice, if she were competent to make it, would be vindicated by the law. Her prognosis is extremely poor - she will never resume cognitive life. And the bodily invasion is very great - she requires 24 hour intensive nursing care, antibiotics, the assistance of a respirator, a catheter and feeding tube.

Our affirmation of Karen's independent right of choice, however, would ordinarily be based upon her competency to assert it. The sad truth, however, is that she is grossly incompetent and we cannot discern her supposed choice based on the testimony of her previous conversation with friends. . . . Nevertheless we have concluded that Karen's right of privacy may be asserted on her behalf by her guardian under the peculiar circumstances here present.

 . . . . The only practical way to prevent destruction of the right [of privacy] is to permit the guardian and family of Karen to render their best judgment, subject to the qualifications hereinafter stated, as to whether she would exercise it in these circumstances. If their conclusion is in the affirmative this decision should be accepted by a society the overwhelming majority of whose members would, we think, in similar circumstances, exercise such a choice in the same way for themselves or for those closest to them. It is for this reason that we determine that Karen's right of privacy may be asserted in her behalf, in this respect, by her guardian and family under the particular circumstances presented by this record.

 . . . . Karen Quinlan is a 22 year old adult. Her right of privacy in respect of the matter before the Court is to be vindicated by Mr. Quinlan as guardian. . . .

The medical obligation is related to standards and practice prevailing in the profession. The physicians in charge of the case . . . declined to withdraw the respirator. That decision was consistent with the proofs below [facts established in the lower court] as to the then existing medical standards and practices.

Under the law as it then stood, Judge Muir was correct in declining to authorize withdrawal of the respirator.

 . . . . We glean from the record here that physicians distinguish between curing the ill and comforting and

easing the dying; that they refuse to treat the curable as if
they were dying or ought to die, and that they have
sometimes refused to treat the hopeless and dying as if
they were curable. In this sense . . . many of them have
refused to inflict an undesired prolongation of the process
of dying on a patient in irreversible condition when it is
clear that such "therapy" offers neither human nor
humane benefit. . . . [I]n light of the situation in the
present case . . . one would have to think that the use of
[a] respirator or [similar] support could be considered
"ordinary" in the context of the possibly curable patient
but "extraordinary" in the context of the forced sustaining
by cardio-respiratory processes of an irreversibly doomed
patient. . . .

Decision-making within health care if it is considered as
an expression of a primary obligation of the physician . . .
should be controlled primarily within the patient-doctor-
family relationship, as indeed was recognized by Judge
Muir. . . .

The evidence in this case convinces us that the focal point
of decision should be the prognosis as to the reasonable
possibility of return to cognitive and sapient life, as
distinguished from the forced continuance of that
biological vegetative existence to which Karen seems to be
doomed.

. . . . Having concluded that there is a right of privacy
that might permit termination of treatment in the
circumstances of this case, we turn to consider the
relationship of the exercise of that right to the criminal
law. We are aware that such termination of treatment
would accelerate Karen's death. The County Prosecutor
and the Attorney General maintain that there would be

criminal liability for such acceleration. Under the statutes of this State, the unlawful killing of another human being is criminal homicide. We conclude that there would be no criminal homicide in the circumstances of this case. We believe, first, that the ensuing death would not be homicide but rather expiration from existing natural causes. Secondly, even if it were to be regarded as homicide, it would not be unlawful.

. . . . There is a real . . . distinction between the unlawful taking of the life of another and the ending of artificial life-support systems as a matter of self-determination.

Furthermore, the exercise of a constitutional right such as we have here found is protected from criminal prosecution. We do not question the State's undoubted power to punish the taking of human life, but that power does not encompass individuals terminating medical treatment pursuant to their right of privacy. . . .

The trial judge . . . refus[ed] to appoint Joseph Quinlan to be guardian of the person and limiting his guardianship to that of the property of his daughter. . . .

The trial court was apparently convinced of the high character of Joseph Quinlan and his general suitability as guardian under other circumstances, describing him as "very sincere, moral, ethical and religious." The court felt, however, that the obligation to concur in the medical care and treatment of his daughter would be a source of anguish to him and would distort his "decision-making processes." We disagree, for we sense from the whole record before us that while Mr. Quinlan feels a natural grief, and understandably sorrows because of the tragedy which has befallen his daughter, his strength of purpose and character far outweighs these sentiments and qualifies him eminently for guardianship of the person as well as the property of his daughter. . . .

We thus arrive at the formulation of the . . . relief which we have concluded is appropriate to this case. Some time has passed since Karen's physical and mental condition was described to the Court. . . . [W]e assume that she is now even more fragile and nearer to death than she was then. Since her present treating physicians may give reconsideration to her present posture in the light of this opinion, and since we are transferring to [Joseph Quinlan] as guardian the choice of the attending physician and therefore other physicians may be in charge of the case who may take a different view from that of the present attending physicians, we herewith declare the following . . . relief on behalf of [Joseph Quinlan]. Upon the concurrence of the guardian and family of Karen, should the responsible attending physicians conclude that there is no reasonable possibility of Karen's ever emerging from her present comatose condition to a cognitive, sapient state and that the life-support apparatus now being administered to Karen should be discontinued, they shall consult with the hospital "Ethics Committee" or like body of the institution in which Karen is then hospitalized. If that consultative body agrees that there is no reasonable possibility of Karen's ever emerging from her present comatose condition to a cognitive, sapient state, the present life-support system may be withdrawn and said action shall be without any civil or criminal liability therefor on the part of any participant, whether guardian, physician, hospital or others. We herewith specifically so hold.

We therefore remand [send back] this record to the trial court to implement . . . the following decisions:

1. To discharge, with the thanks of the Court for his service, the present guardian of the person of Karen Quinlan, Thomas R. Curtin, Esq., a member of the Bar and an officer of the court.

2. To appoint Joseph Quinlan as guardian of the person of Karen Quinlan with full power to make decisions with regard to the identity of her treating physicians. . . .

Karen Ann Quinlan was removed from the respirator in January 1984. She died on June 11, 1985.

THE U.S. CONSTITUTION

THE U.S. CONSTITUTION

PREAMBLE

We the people of the United States, in order to form a more perfect union, establish justice, insure domestic tranquility, provide for the common defense, promote the general welfare, and secure the blessings of liberty to ourselves and our posterity, do ordain and establish this Constitution for the United States of America.

ARTICLE I

Section 1. All legislative powers herein granted shall be vested in a Congress of the United States, which shall consist of a Senate and House of Representatives.

Section 2. (1) The House of Representatives shall be composed of members chosen every second year by the people of the several states, and the electors in each state shall have the qualifications requisite for electors of the most numerous branch of the State Legislature.

(2) No person shall be a Representative who shall not have attained to the age of twenty-five years, and been seven years a citizen of the United States, and who shall not, when elected, be an inhabitant of that state in which he shall be chosen.

(3) Representatives and direct taxes shall be apportioned among the several states which may be included within this union, according to their respective numbers, which shall be determined by adding to the whole number of free persons, including those bound to service for a term of years, and excluding Indians not taxed, three-fifths of all other persons. The actual enumeration shall be made

within three years after the first meeting of the Congress
of the United States, and within every subsequent term of
ten years, in such manner as they shall by law direct. The
number of Representatives shall not exceed one for every
thirty thousand, but each state shall have at least one Representative; and until such enumeration shall be made, the
State of New Hampshire shall be entitled to choose three,
Massachusetts eight, Rhode Island and Providence Planta-
tions one, Connecticut five, New York six, New Jersey
four, Pennsylvania eight, Delaware one, Maryland six, Virginia ten, North Carolina five, South Carolina five, and
Georgia three.

(4) When vacancies happen in the representation from
any state, the executive authority thereof shall issue writs
of election to fill such vacancies.

(5) The House of Representatives shall choose their
Speaker and other Officers; and shall have the sole power
of impeachment.

Section 3. (1) The Senate of the United States shall be
composed of two Senators from each state, chosen by the
legislature thereof, for six years; and each Senator shall
have one vote.

(2) Immediately after they shall be assembled in consequence of the first election, they shall be divided as equally as may be into three classes. The seats of the Senators
of the first class shall be vacated at the expiration of the
second year, of the second class at the expiration of the
fourth year, and of the third class at the expiration of the
sixth year, so that one-third may be chosen every second
year; and if vacancies happen by resignation, or otherwise,
during the recess of the legislature of any state, the execu-

tive thereof may make temporary appointments until the next meeting of the legislature, which shall then fill such vacancies.

(3) No person shall be a Senator who shall not have attained to the age of thirty years, and been nine years a citizen of the United States, and who shall not, when elected, be an inhabitant of that state for which he shall be chosen.

(4) The Vice President of the United States shall be President of the Senate, but shall have no vote, unless they be equally divided.

(5) The Senate shall choose their other Officers, and also a President pro tempore, in the absence of the Vice President, or when he shall exercise the Office of President of the United States.

(6) The Senate shall have the sole power to try all impeachments. When sitting for that purpose, they shall be on oath or affirmation. When the President of the United States is tried, the Chief Justice shall preside: and no person shall be convicted without the concurrence of two-thirds of the members present.

(7) Judgment in cases of impeachment shall not extend further than to removal from office, and disqualification to hold and enjoy any office of honor, trust, or profit under the United States: but the party convicted shall nevertheless be liable and subject to indictment, trial, judgment, and punishment, according to law.

Section 4. (1) The times, places and manner of holding elections for Senators and Representatives, shall be prescribed in each state by the legislature thereof; but the Congress may at any time by law make or alter such regulations, except as to the places of choosing Senators.

(2) The Congress shall assemble at least once in every year, and such meeting shall be on the first Monday in December, unless they shall by law appoint a different day.

Section 5. (1) Each House shall be the judge of the elections, returns, and qualifications of its own members, and a majority of each shall constitute a quorum to do business; but a smaller number may adjourn from day to day, and may be authorized to compel the attendance of absent members, in such manner, and under such penalties as each House may provide.

(2) Each House may determine the rules of its proceedings, punish its members for disorderly behavior, and, with the concurrence of two-thirds, expel a member.

(3) Each House shall keep a journal of its proceedings, and from time to time publish the same, excepting such parts as may in their judgment require secrecy; and the yeas and nays of the members of either House on any question shall, at the desire of one-fifth of those present, be entered on the journal.

(4) Neither House, during the Session of Congress, shall, without the consent of the other, adjourn for more than three days, nor to any other place than that in which the two Houses shall be sitting.

Section 6. (1) The Senators and Representatives shall receive a compensation for their services, to be ascertained by law, and paid out of the Treasury of the United States. They shall in all cases, except treason, felony and breach of the peace, be privileged from arrest during their attendance at the session of their respective Houses, and in going to and returning from the same; and for any speech or debate in either House, they shall not be questioned in any other place.

(2) No Senator or Representative shall, during the time for which he was elected, be appointed to any civil office under the authority of the United States, which shall have been created, or the emoluments whereof shall have been increased during such time and no person holding any office under the United States, shall be a member of either House during his continuance in office.

Section 7. (1) All bills for raising revenue shall originate in the House of Representatives; but the Senate may propose or concur with amendments as on other bills.

(2) Every bill which shall have passed the House of Representatives and the Senate, shall, before it become a law, be presented to the President of the United States; if he approve he shall sign it, but if not he shall return it, with his objections to the House in which it shall have originated, who shall enter the objections at large on their journal, and proceed to reconsider it. If after such reconsideration two-thirds of that House shall agree to pass the bill, it shall be sent together with the objections, to the other House, by which it shall likewise be reconsidered, and if approved by two-thirds of that House, it shall become a law. But in all such cases the votes of both Houses shall be determined by yeas and nays, and the names of the per-

sons voting for and against the bill shall be entered on the journal of each House respectively. If any bill shall not be returned by the President within ten days (Sundays excepted) after it shall have been presented to him, the same shall be a law, in like manner as if he had signed it, unless the Congress by their adjournment prevent its return in which case it shall not be a law.

(3) Every order, resolution, or vote, to which the concurrence of the Senate and House of Representatives may be necessary (except on a question of adjournment) shall be presented to the President of the United States; and before the same shall take effect, shall be approved by him, or being disapproved by him, shall be repassed by two-thirds of the Senate and House of Representatives, according to the rules and limitations prescribed in the case of a bill.

Section 8. (1) The Congress shall have the power to lay and collect taxes, duties, imposts and excises, to pay the debts and provide for the common defense and general welfare of the United States; but all duties, imposts and excises shall be uniform throughout the United States;

(2) To borrow money on the credit of the United States;

(3) To regulate commerce with foreign nations, and among the several states, and with the Indian Tribes;

(4) To establish an uniform Rule of Naturalization, and uniform laws on the subject of bankruptcies throughout the United States;

(5) To coin money, regulate the value thereof, and of foreign coin, and fix the standard of weights and measures;

(6) To provide for the punishment of counterfeiting the securities and current coin of the United States;

(7) To establish Post Offices and Post Roads;

(8) To promote the progress of science and useful arts, by securing for limited times to authors and inventors the exclusive right to their respective writings and discoveries;

(9) To constitute tribunals inferior to the Supreme Court;

(10) To define and punish piracies and felonies committed on the high seas, and offenses against the Law of Nations;

(11) To declare war, grant Letters of marque and reprisal, and make rules concerning captures on land and water;

(12) To raise and support armies, but no appropriation of money to that use shall be for a longer term than two years;

(13) To provide and maintain a Navy;

(14) To make rules for the government and regulation of the land and naval forces;

(15) To provide for calling forth the Militia to execute the laws of the Union, suppress insurrections and repel invasions;

(16) To provide for organizing, arming, and disciplining, the Militia, and for governing such part of them as may be employed in the service of the United States, reserving to the states respectively, the appointment of the Officers,

and the authority of training the Militia according to the discipline prescribed by Congress;

(17) To exercise exclusive legislation in all cases whatsoever, over such district (not exceeding ten miles square) as may, by cession of particular states, and the acceptance of Congress, become the Seat of the Government of the United States, and to exercise like authority over all places purchased by the consent of the legislature of the state in which the same shall be, for the erection of forts, magazines, arsenals, dockyards, and other needful buildings; - and

(18) To make all laws which shall be necessary and proper for carrying into execution the foregoing powers, and all other powers vested by this Constitution in the Government of the United States, or in any Department or Officer thereof.

Section 9. (1) The migration or importation of such persons as any of the states now existing shall think proper to admit, shall not be prohibited by the Congress prior to the year one thousand eight hundred and eight, but a tax or duty may be imposed on such importation, not exceeding ten dollars for each person.

(2) The privilege of the writ of habeas corpus shall not be suspended, unless when in cases of rebellion or invasion the public safety may require it.

(3) No bill of attainder or ex post facto law shall be passed.

(4) No capitation, or other direct, tax shall be laid, unless in proportion to the census or enumeration herein before directed to be taken.

(5) No tax or duty shall be laid on articles exported from any state.

(6) No preference shall be given by any regulation of commerce or revenue to the ports of one state over those of another: nor shall vessels bound to, or from, one state be obliged to enter, clear, or pay duties in another.

(7) No money shall be drawn from the Treasury, but in consequence of appropriations made by law; and a regular statement and account of the receipts and expenditures of all public money shall be published from time to time.

(8) No title of nobility shall be granted by the United States: and no person holding any office of profit or trust under them, shall, without the consent of the Congress, accept of any present, emolument, office, or title, of any kind whatever, from any King, Prince, or foreign State.

Section 10. (1) No state shall enter into any treaty, alliance, or confederation; grant letters of marque and reprisal; coin money; emit bills of credit; make any thing but gold and silver coin a tender in payment of debts; pass any bill of attainder, ex post facto law, or law impairing the obligation of contracts, or grant any title of nobility.

(2) No state shall, without the consent of the Congress, lay any imposts or duties on imports or exports, except what may be absolutely necessary for executing its inspection laws: and the net produce of all duties and imposts, laid by any state on imports or exports, shall be for the use of

the Treasury of the United States; and all such laws shall be subject to the revision and control of the Congress.

(3) No state shall, without the consent of Congress, lay any duty of tonnage, keep troops, or ships of war in time of peace, enter into any agreement or compact with another state, or with a foreign power, or engage in war, unless actually invaded, or in such imminent danger as will not admit of delay.

ARTICLE II

Section 1. (1) The executive power shall be vested in a President of the United States of America. He shall hold his office during the term of four years, and, together with the Vice President, chosen for the same term, be elected, as follows:

(2) Each state shall appoint, in such manner as the legislature thereof may direct, a number of electors, equal to the whole number of Senators and Representatives to which the state may be entitled in the Congress; but no Senator or Representative, or person holding an office of trust or profit under the United States, shall be appointed an Elector.

(3) The electors shall meet in their respective states, and vote by ballot for two persons, of whom one at least shall not be an inhabitant of the same state with themselves. And they shall make a list of all the persons voted for, and of the number of votes for each; which list they shall sign and certify, and transmit sealed to the Seat of the Government of the United States, directed to the President of the Senate. The President of the Senate shall, in the presence of the Senate and House of Representatives,

open all the certificates, and the votes shall then be counted. The person having the greatest number of votes shall be the President, if such number be a majority of the whole number of electors appointed; and if there be more than one who have such majority, and have an equal number of votes, then the House of Representatives shall immediately choose by ballot one of them for President; and if no person have a majority, then from the five highest on the list the said House shall in like manner choose the President. But in choosing the President, the votes shall be taken by states the representation from each state having one vote; a quorum for this purpose shall consist of a member or members from two-thirds of the states, and a majority of all the states shall be necessary to a choice. In every case, after the choice of the President, the person having the greater number of votes of the electors shall be the Vice President. But if there should remain two or more who have equal votes, the Senate shall choose from them by ballot the Vice President.

(4) The Congress may determine the time of choosing the Electors, and the day on which they shall give their votes; which day shall be the same throughout the United States.

(5) No person except a natural born citizen, or a citizen of the United States, at the time of the adoption of this Constitution, shall be eligible to the Office of President; neither shall any person be eligible to that Office who shall not have attained to the age of thirty-five years, and been fourteen years a resident within the United States.

(6) In case of the removal of the President from Office, or of his death, resignation or inability to discharge the powers and duties of the said Office, the same shall devolve on the Vice President, and the Congress may by law

provide for the case of removal, death, resignation or inability, both of the President and Vice President, declaring
what Officer shall then act as President, and such Officer
shall act accordingly, until the disability be removed, or a
President shall be elected.

(7) The President shall, at stated times, receive for his
services, a compensation, which shall neither be increased
nor diminished during the period for which he shall have
been elected, and he shall not receive within that period
any other emolument from the United States, or any of
them.

(8) Before he enter on the execution of his office, he shall
take the following oath or affirmation: "I do solemnly
swear (or affirm) that I will faithfully execute the Office
of President of the United States, and will to the best of
my ability, preserve, protect and defend the Constitution
of the United States."

Section 2. (1) The President shall be Commander in Chief
of the Army and Navy of the United States, and of the
militia of the several states, when called into the actual
service of the United States; he may require the opinion,
in writing, of the principal Officer in each of the Executive Departments, upon any subject relating to the duties
of their respective Offices, and he shall have power to
grant reprieves and pardons for offenses against the United States, except in cases of impeachment.

(2) He shall have power, by and with the advice and consent of the Senate to make treaties, provided two-thirds of
the Senators present concur; and he shall nominate, and
by and with the advice and consent of the Senate, shall appoint Ambassadors, other public Ministers and Consuls,

Judges of the supreme Court, and all other Officers of the United States, whose appointments are not herein otherwise provided for, and which shall be established by law; but the Congress may by law vest the appointment of such inferior Officers, as they think proper, in the President alone, in the courts of law, or in the heads of departments.

(3) The President shall have power to fill up all vacancies that may happen during the recess of the Senate, by granting commissions which shall expire at the end of their next session.

Section 3. He shall from time to time give to the Congress information of the State of the Union, and recommend to their consideration such measures as he shall judge necessary and expedient; he may, on extraordinary occasions, convene both Houses, or either of them, and in case of disagreement between them, with respect to the time of adjournment, he may adjourn them to such time as he shall think proper; he shall receive Ambassadors and other public Ministers; he shall take care that the laws be faithfully executed, and shall commission all the Officers of the United States.

Section 4. The President, Vice President and all civil Officers of the United States, shall be removed from office on impeachment for, and conviction of, treason, bribery, or other high crimes and misdemeanors.

ARTICLE III

Section 1. The judicial power of the United States, shall be vested in one supreme Court, and in such inferior courts as the Congress may from time to time ordain and establish. The Judges, both of the supreme and inferior courts, shall hold their Offices during good behaviour, and shall, at stated times, receive for their services a compensation, which shall not be diminished during their continuance in office.

Section 2. (1) The judicial power shall extend to all cases, in law and equity, arising under this Constitution, the laws of the United States, and treaties made, or which shall be made, under their authority; - to all cases affecting Ambassadors, other public Ministers and Consuls; - to all cases of admiralty and maritime jurisdiction; - to controversies to which the United States shall be a party; - to controversies between two or more states; - between a state and citizens of another state; - between citizens of different states; - between citizens of the same state claiming lands under the grants of different states, and between a state, or the citizens thereof, and foreign states, citizens or subjects.

(2) In all cases affecting Ambassadors, other public Ministers and Consuls, and those in which a state shall be a party, the supreme Court shall have original jurisdiction. In all the other cases before mentioned, the supreme Court shall have appellate jurisdiction, both as to law and fact, with such exceptions, and under such regulations as the Congress shall make.

(3) The trial of all crimes, except in cases of impeachment, shall be by jury; and such trial shall be held in the state where the said crimes shall have been committed; but when not committed within any state, the trial shall be at such place or places as the Congress may by law have directed.

Section 3. (1) Treason against the United States, shall consist only in levying war against them, or, in adhering to their enemies, giving them aid and comfort. No person shall be convicted of treason unless on the testimony of two witnesses to the same overt act, or on confession in open Court.

(2) The Congress shall have power to declare the punishment of treason, but no Attainder of Treason shall work corruption of blood, or forfeiture except during the life of the person attainted.

ARTICLE IV

Section 1. Full faith and credit shall be given in each state to the public acts, records, and judicial proceedings of every other state. And the Congress may by general laws prescribe the manner in which such acts, records and proceedings shall be proved, and the effect thereof.

Section 2. (1) The citizens of each state shall be entitled to all privileges and immunities of citizens in the several states.

(2) A person charged in any state with treason, felony, or other crime, who shall flee from justice, and be found in another state, shall on demand of the executive authority of the state from which he fled, be delivered up, to be removed to the state having jurisdiction of the crime.

(3) No person held to service or labor in one state, under the laws thereof, escaping into another, shall, in consequence of any law or regulation therein, be discharged from such service or labor, but shall be delivered up on

claim of the party to whom such service or labor may be due.

Section 3. (1) New states may be admitted by the Congress into this union; but no new state shall be formed or erected within the jurisdiction of any other state; nor any state be formed by the junction of two or more states, or parts of states, without the consent of the legislatures of the states concerned as well as of the Congress.

(2) The Congress shall have power to dispose of and make all needful rules and regulations respecting the territory or other property belonging to the United States; and nothing in this Constitution shall be so construed as to prejudice any claims of the United States, or of any particular state.

Section 4. The United States shall guarantee to every state in this union a Republican form of government, and shall protect each of them against invasion; and on application of the legislature, or of the executive (when the legislature cannot be convened) against domestic violence.

ARTICLE V

The Congress, whenever two-thirds of both Houses shall deem it necessary, shall propose amendments to this Constitution, or, on the application of the legislatures of two-thirds of the several states, shall call a convention for proposing amendments, which, in either case, shall be valid to all intents and purposes, as part of this constitution, when ratified by the legislatures of three-fourths of the several states, or by conventions in three-fourths thereof, as the one or the other mode of ratification may be proposed by the Congress; provided that no amendment which may be made prior to the year one thousand eight hundred and eight shall in any manner affect the first and fourth clauses in the Ninth Section of the first Article; and that no state, without its consent, shall be deprived of its equal suffrage in the Senate.

ARTICLE VI

(1) All debts contracted and engagements entered into, before the adoption of this Constitution shall be as valid against the United States under this Constitution, as under the Confederation.

(2) This Constitution, and the laws of the United States which shall be made in pursuance thereof; and all treaties made, or which shall be made, under the authority of the United States, shall be the supreme law of the land; and the Judges in every state shall be bound thereby, any thing in the Constitution or laws of any state to the contrary notwithstanding.

(3) The Senators and Representatives before mentioned, and the Members of the several State Legislatures, and all executive and judicial Officers, both of the United States and of the several states, shall be bound by oath or affirmation, to support this Constitution; but no religious test shall ever be required as a qualification to any office or public trust under the United States.

ARTICLE VII

The ratification of the Conventions of nine states shall be sufficient for the establishment of this Constitution between the states so ratifying the same.

AMENDMENT I (1791)

Congress shall make no law respecting an establishment of religion, or prohibiting the free exercise thereof; or abridging the freedom of speech, or of the press; or the right of the people peaceably to assemble, and to petition the Government for a redress of grievances.

AMENDMENT II (1791)

A well regulated Militia, being necessary to the security of a free state, the right of the people to keep and bear arms, shall not be infringed.

AMENDMENT III (1791)

No soldier shall, in time of peace be quartered in any house, without the consent of the owner, nor in time of war, but in a manner to be prescribed by law.

AMENDMENT IV (1791)

The right of the people to be secure in their persons, houses, papers, and effects, against unreasonable searches and seizures, shall not be violated, and no warrants shall issue, but upon probable cause, supported by oath or affirmation, and particularly describing the place to be searched, and the persons or things to be seized.

AMENDMENT V (1791)

No person shall be held to answer for a capital, or otherwise infamous crime, unless on a presentment or indictment of a Grand Jury, except in cases arising in the land or naval forces, or in the Militia, when in actual service in time of war or public danger; nor shall any person be subject for the same offense to be twice put in jeopardy of life or limb; nor shall be compelled in any criminal case to be a witness against himself, nor be deprived of life, liberty, or property, without due process of law; nor shall private property be taken for public use, without just compensation.

AMENDMENT VI (1791)

In all criminal prosecutions, the accused shall enjoy the right to a speedy and public trial, by an impartial jury of the state and district wherein the crime shall have been committed, which district shall have been previously ascertained by law, and to be informed of the nature and cause of the accusation; to be confronted with the witnesses against him; to have compulsory process for obtaining witnesses in his favor, and to have the assistance of counsel for his defense.

AMENDMENT VII (1791)

In suits at common law, where the value in controversy shall exceed twenty dollars, the right of trial by jury shall be preserved, and no fact tried by jury, shall be otherwise re-examined in any court of the United States, than according to the rules of the common law.

AMENDMENT VIII (1791)

Excessive bail shall not be required, nor excessive fines imposed, nor cruel and unusual punishments inflicted.

AMENDMENT IX (1791)

The enumeration in the Constitution, of certain rights, shall not be construed to deny or disparage others retained by the people.

AMENDMENT X (1791)

The powers not delegated to the United States by the Constitution, nor prohibited by it to the States, are reserved to the States respectively, or to the people.

AMENDMENT XI (1798)

The judicial power of the United States shall not be construed to extend to any suit in law or equity, commenced or prosecuted against one of the United States by citizens of another state, or by citizens or subjects of any foreign state.

AMENDMENT XII (1804)

The Electors shall meet in their respective states and vote by ballot for President and Vice-President, one of whom, at least, shall not be an inhabitant of the same state with themselves; they shall name in their ballots the person voted for as President, and in distinct ballots the person voted for as Vice-President, and they shall make distinct lists of all persons voted for as President, and of all persons voted for as Vice-President, and of the number of votes for each, which lists they shall sign and certify, and transmit sealed to the seat of the government of the United States, directed to the President of the Senate; - the President of the Senate shall, in the presence of the Senate and House of Representatives, open all the certificates and the votes shall then be counted; - the person having the greatest number of votes for President, shall be the President, if such number be a majority of the whole number of electors appointed; and if no person have such majority, then from the persons having the highest numbers not exceeding three on the list of those voted for as President, the House of Representatives shall choose immediately, by ballot, the President. But in choosing the President, the votes shall be taken by states, the representation from each state having one vote; a quorum for this purpose shall consist of a member or members from two-thirds of the states, and a majority of all the states shall be necessary to a choice. And if the House of Representatives shall not choose a President whenever the right of choice shall devolve upon them before the fourth day of March next following, then the Vice-President shall act as President, as in the case of the death or other constitutional disability of the President. - The person having the greatest number of votes as Vice-President, shall be the Vice-President, if such number be a majority of the whole number of Electors appointed, and if no person have a majority, then from the two highest numbers on the list, the Senate shall choose the Vice-President; a quorum for the purpose shall consist of two-thirds of the whole number of Senators, and a majority of the whole number shall be necessary to a choice. But no person constitutionally ineligible to the office of President shall be eligible to that of Vice-President of the United States.

AMENDMENT XIII (1865)

Section 1. Neither slavery nor involuntary servitude, except as a punishment for crime whereof the party shall have been duly convicted, shall exist within the United States, or any place subject to their jurisdiction.

Section 2. Congress shall have power to enforce this article by appropriate legislation.

AMENDMENT XIV (1868)

Section 1. All persons born or naturalized in the United States, and subject to the jurisdiction thereof, are citizens of the United States and of the state wherein they reside. No state shall make or enforce any law which shall abridge the privileges or immunities of citizens of the United States; nor shall any state deprive any person of life, liberty, or property, without due process of law; nor deny to any person within its jurisdiction the equal protection of the laws.

Section 2. Representatives shall be apportioned among the several states according to their respective numbers, counting the whole number of persons in each State excluding Indians not taxed. But when the right to vote at any election for the choice of electors for President and Vice President of the United States, Representatives in Congress, the Executive and Judicial officers of a state, or the members of the Legislature thereof, is denied to any of the male inhabitants of such state, being twenty-one years of age, and citizens of the United States, or in any way abridged, except for participation in rebellion, or other crime, the basis of representation therein shall be reduced in the proportion which the number of such male citizens shall bear to the whole number of male citizens twenty-one years of age in such state.

Section 3. No person shall be a Senator or Representative in Congress, or elector of President and Vice President, or hold any office, civil or military, under the United States, or under any state, who having previously taken an oath, as a member of Congress, or as an officer of the United States, or as a member of any state legislature, or as an executive or judicial officer of any state, to support the Constitution of the United States, shall have engaged in insurrection or rebellion against the same, or given aid or comfort to the enemies thereof. But Congress may by a vote of two-thirds of each House, remove such disability.

Section 4. The validity of the public debt of the United States, authorized by law, including debts incurred for payment of pensions and bounties for services in suppressing insurrection or rebellion, shall not be questioned. But neither the United States nor any state shall assume or pay any debt or obligation incurred in aid of insurrection or rebellion against the United States, or any claim for the loss or emancipation of any slave; but all such debts, obligations and claims shall be held illegal and void.

Section 5. The Congress shall have power to enforce, by appropriate legislation, the provisions of this article.

AMENDMENT XV (1870)

Section 1. The right of citizens of the United States to vote shall not be denied or abridged by the United States or by any state on account of race, color, or previous condition of servitude.

Section 2. The Congress shall have power to enforce this article by appropriate legislation.

AMENDMENT XVI (1913)

The Congress shall have power to lay and collect taxes on incomes, from whatever source derived, without apportionment among the several states, and without regard to any census or enumeration.

AMENDMENT XVII (1913)

(1) The Senate of the United States shall be composed of two Senators from each state, elected by the people thereof, for six years; and each Senator shall have one vote. The electors in each State shall have the qualifications requisite for electors of the most numerous branch of the state legislatures.

(2) When vacancies happen in the representation of any state in the Senate, the executive authority of such state shall issue writs of election to fill such vacancies: *provided,* that the legislature of any state may empower the executive thereof to make temporary appointments until the people fill the vacancies by election as the legislature may direct.

(3) This amendment shall not be so construed as to affect the election or term of any Senator chosen before it becomes valid as part of the Constitution.

AMENDMENT XVIII (1919)

Section 1. After one year from the ratification of this article the manufacture, sale, or transportation of intoxicating liquors within, the importation thereof into, or the exportation thereof from the United States and all territory subject to the jurisdiction thereof for beverage purposes is hereby prohibited.

Section 2. The Congress and the several states shall have concurrent power to enforce this article by appropriate legislation.

Section 3. This article shall be inoperative unless it shall have been ratified as an amendment to the Constitution by the legislatures of the several states, as provided in the Constitution, within seven years from the date of the submission hereof to the states by the Congress.

AMENDMENT XIX (1920)

(1) The right of citizens of the United States to vote shall not be denied or abridged by the United States or by any state on account of sex.

(2) Congress shall have power to enforce this article by appropriate legislation.

AMENDMENT XX (1933)

Section 1. The terms of the President and Vice President shall end at noon on the 20th day of January, and the terms of Senators and Representatives at noon on the 3d day of January, of the years in which such terms would have ended if this article had not been ratified; and the terms of their successors shall then begin.

Section 2. The Congress shall assemble at least once in every year, and such meeting shall begin at noon on the 3d day of January, unless they shall by law appoint a different day.

Section 3. If, at the time fixed for the beginning of the term of the President, the President elect shall have died, the Vice President elect shall become President. If the President shall not have been chosen before the time fixed for the beginning of his term, or if the President elect shall have failed to qualify, then the Vice President elect shall act as President until a President shall have qualified; and the Congress may by law provide for the case wherein neither a President elect nor a Vice President elect shall have qualified, declaring who shall then act as President, or the manner in which one who is to act shall be selected, and such person shall act accordingly until a President or Vice President shall have qualified.

Section 4. The Congress may by law provide for the case of the death of any of the persons from whom the House of Representatives may choose a President whenever the right of choice shall have devolved upon them, and for the case of the death of any of the persons from whom the Senate may choose a Vice President whenever the right of choice shall have devolved upon them.

Section 5. Sections 1 and 2 shall take effect on the 15th day of October following the ratification of this article.

Section 6. This article shall be inoperative unless it shall have been ratified as an amendment to the Constitution by the legislatures of three-fourths of the several states within seven years from the date of its submission.

AMENDMENT XXI (1933)

Section 1. The eighteenth article of amendment to the Constitution of the United States is hereby repealed.

Section 2. The transportation or importation into any state, territory, or possession of the United States for delivery or use therein of intoxicating liquors, in violation of the laws thereof, is hereby prohibited.

Section 3. This article shall be inoperative unless it shall have been ratified as an amendment to the Constitution by conventions in the several states, as provided in the Constitution, within seven years from the date of the submission hereof to the states by the Congress.

AMENDMENT XXII (1951)

Section 1. No person shall be elected to the office of the President more than twice, and no person who has held the office of President, or acted as President, for more than two years of a term to which some other person was elected President shall be elected to the office of President more than once. But this Article shall not apply to any person holding the office of President when this Article was proposed by the Congress, and shall not prevent any person who may be holding the office of President, or acting as President, during the term within which this Article becomes operative from holding the office of President or acting as President during the remainder of such term.

Section 2. This article shall be inoperative unless it shall have been ratified as an amendment to the Constitution by the legislatures of three-fourths of the several states within seven years from the date of its submission to the states by the Congress.

AMENDMENT XXIII (1961)

Section 1. The District constituting the seat of Government of the United States shall appoint in such manner as the Congress may direct:

A number of electors of President and Vice President equal to the whole number of Senators and Representatives in Congress to which the District would be entitled if it were a state, but in no event more than the least populous state; they shall be in addition to those appointed by the states, but they shall be considered, for the purposes of the election of President and Vice President, to be electors appointed by a state; and they shall meet in the District and perform such duties as provided by the twelfth article of amendment.

Section 2. The Congress shall have power to enforce this article by appropriate legislation.

AMENDMENT XXIV (1964)

Section 1. The right of citizens of the United States to vote in any primary or other election for President or Vice President, for electors for President or Vice President, or for Senator or Representative in Congress, shall not be denied or abridged by the United States, or any state by reason of failure to pay any poll tax or other tax.

Section 2. The Congress shall have power to enforce this article by appropriate legislation.

AMENDMENT XXV (1967)

Section 1. In case of the removal of the President from office or of his death or resignation, the Vice President shall become President.

Section 2. Whenever there is a vacancy in the office of the Vice President, the President shall nominate a Vice President who shall take office upon confirmation by a majority vote of both Houses of Congress.

Section 3. Whenever the President transmits to the President pro tempore of the Senate and the Speaker of the House of Representatives his written declaration that he is unable to discharge the powers and duties of his office, and until he transmits to them a written declaration to the contrary, such powers and duties shall be discharged by the Vice President as Acting President.

Section 4. Whenever the Vice President and a majority of either the principal officers of the executive departments or of such other body as Congress may by law provide, transmit to the President pro tempore of the Senate and the Speaker of the House of Representatives their written declaration that the President is unable to discharge the powers and duties of his office, the Vice President shall immediately assume the powers and duties of the office as Acting President.

Thereafter, when the President transmits to the President pro tempore of the Senate and the Speaker of the House of Representatives his written declaration that no inability exists, he shall resume the powers and duties of his office unless the Vice President and a majority of either the principal officers of the executive department or of such other body as Congress may by law provide, transmit within four days to the President pro tempore of the Senate and the Speaker of the House of Representatives their written declaration and the President is unable to discharge the powers and duties of his office. Thereupon Congress shall decide the issue, assembling within forty-eight hours for that purpose if not in session. If the Congress, within twenty-one days after receipt of the latter written declaration, or, if Congress is not in session, within twenty-one days after Congress is required to assemble, determines by two-thirds vote of both Houses that the President is unable to discharge the power and duties of his office, the Vice President shall continue to discharge the same as Acting President; otherwise, the President shall resume the powers and duties of his office.

AMENDMENT XXVI (1971)

Section 1. The right of citizens of the United States, who are eighteen years of age or older, to vote shall not be denied or abridged by the United States or by any state on account of age.

Section 2. The Congress shall have power to enforce this article by appropriate legislation.

BIBLIOGRAPHY

SLAVERY

Brooke, J.T., *Short Notes on the Dred Scott Case*, Cincinnati: Moore, Wilstach, Keys & Co., 1861.

Ehrlich, Walter, *They Have No Rights: Dred Scott's Struggle for Freedom*, New York: Greenwood Press, 1979.

Fehrenbacher, Don, *Slavery, Law & Politics: The Dred Scott Case in Historical Perspective*, New York: Oxford University Press, 1981.

Stewart, James B., *Holy Warriors: The Abolitionists and American Slavery*, New York: Hill & Wang, 1976.

Wilson, Charles Morrow, *The Dred Scott Decision*, Philadelphia: Auerbach Publishers, 1973.

WOMEN'S SUFFRAGE

Anthony, Susan B., *An Account of the Proceedings on the Trial of Susan B. Anthony, on the Charge of Illegal Voting, at the Presidential Election in November, 1872*, New York: Arno Press, 1974.

Dorr, Rheta, *Susan B. Anthony: The Woman Who Changed the Mind of a Nation*, New York: AMS Pr., 1928 (reprinted 1974).

Flexner, Eleanor, *Century of Struggle: The Women's Rights Movement in the United States*, Cambridge: Harvard University Press, 1975.

Lutz, Alma, *Susan B. Anthony: Rebel, Crusader, Humanitarian*, Washington, DC: Zenger Publishing, 1959 (reprinted 1976).

Magrath, C. Peter, *Morrison Waite: The Triumph of Character*, Macmillan, 1963.

Stanton, Elizabeth C., Susan B. Anthony, and Matilda J. Gage, *History of Woman Suffrage*, New York: Fowler & Wells, 1881.

JAPANESE AMERICAN CONCENTRATION CAMPS

Daniels, Roger, *Concentration Camps: North American Japanese in the United States & Canada During World War II*, Melbourne: Krieger Publishing Co., 1981.

Grodzins, Morton, *Americans Betrayed: Politics and the Japanese Evacuation*, Chicago: University of Chicago Press, 1949.

Irons, Peter, ed., *Justice Delayed: The Record of the Japanese American Internment Cases*, Middleton: Wesleyan University Press, 1989.

Rostow, Eugene V., *The Japanese American Cases - A Disaster*, New Haven: Yale Law Journal 54: 489-533 (1989).

BIBLE READING
IN THE PUBLIC SCHOOLS

Dolbeare, Kenneth M., and Phillip E. Hammond, *The School Prayer Decisions From Court Policy to Local Practice*, Chicago: University of Chicago Press, 1971.

Pfeffer, Leo, *Church, State and Freedom*, Boston: Beacon Press, 1967.

Stokes, A.P., and Leo Pfeffer, *Church and State in the United States*, New York: Harper & Row, 1964.

THE BOOK BANNED IN BOSTON

Friedman, Leon, comp., *Obscenity; The Complete Oral Arguments Before the Supreme Court in the Major Obscenity Cases*, New York: Chelsea House Publishers, 1970.

Rembar, Charles, *The End of Obscenity: The Trials of Lady Chatterley, Tropic of Cancer, and Fanny Hill*, New York: Harper & Row, 1986.

RIGHTS OF THE ACCUSED

Kamisar, Yale, *Police Interrogations and Confessions*, Ann Arbor: University of Michigan Press, 1980.

Medalie, Richard James, *From Escobedo to Miranda: The Anatomy of a Supreme Court Decision*, Washington, D.C.: Lerner Law Book Co., 1966.

THE DEATH PENALTY

Bedau, Hugo A., ed., *The Death Penalty in America*, New York: Oxford University Press, 1982.

Stevens, Leonard A., *Death Penalty: The Case of Life vs. Death in the United States*, New York: Coward, McCann & Geoghegan, 1978.

Van den Haag, Ernest, *The Death Penalty: A Debate*, New York: Plenum Press, 1983.

HOMOSEXUALITY

Massari, Angelina Marie, "The Supreme Court Gives States a Free Rein with Sodomy Statutes: Bowers v. Hardwick," *Washington University Journal of Urban and Contemporary Law*, Vol. 31 (1987).

OFFENSIVE SPEECH

Nimmer, Melville B., "The Meaning of Symbolic Speech to the First Amendment," *UCLA Law Review* 21: 29-62.

Post, Robert C., "The Constitutional Concept of Public Discourse: Outrageous Opinion, Democratic Deliberation, and Hustler Magazine v. Falwell," *Harvard Law Review*, Vol. 103, No. 3 (Jan. 1990).

Smolla, Rodney A., *Jerry Falwell v. Larry Flynt: The First Amendment on Trial*, New York: St. Martin's Press, 1988.

THE RIGHT TO DIE

Colen, B.D., *Karen Ann Quinlan: Dying in the Age of Eternal Life*, New York: Nash Pub., 1976.

Quinlan, Joseph, *Karen Ann: The Quinlans Tell Their Story*, Garden City: Doubleday, 1977.

"To Die With Dignity," *Time*, vol. 137 (January 7, 1991), p. 59.

THE SUPREME COURT

Agresto, John, *The Supreme Court and Constitutional Democracy*, Ithaca: Cornell University Press, 1984.

Cox, Archibald, *The Court and the Constitution*, New York: Houghton-Mifflin, 1988.

Dumbauld, Edward, *The Bill of Rights and What It Means Today*, New York: Greenwood Press, 1979.

Goode, Stephen, *The Controversial Court: Supreme Court Influences on American Life*, New York: Messner, 1982.

Lawson, Don, *Landmark Supreme Court Cases*, Hillside: Enslow Publishers, Inc., 1987.

Rehnquist, William H., *The Supreme Court: How It Was, How It Is*, New York: Morrow, 1987.

Woodward, Bob, and Scott Armstrong, *The Brethren: Inside the Supreme Court*, New York: Simon & Schuster, 1979.

Yudof, Mark, *When Government Speaks: Politics, Law, and Government Expression in America*, Berkeley and Los Angeles: University of California Press, 1983.

INDEX

ACLU, see American Civil Liberties Union
Act of Congress (1942) 50-52, 56, 60
American Civil Liberties Union 65
Arizona 96, 112
Article I, U.S. Constitution 45
Articles of Confederation 26-27, 31, 120
Assembly centers 56-58
"Best interest" standard 164
Bill of Rights 75, 81, 120, 137, 185
Bingham, Congressman 118
Bill of Rights, English 119-120
Black, Justice Hugo 50-51, 76, 78
Blackmun, Justice 127
Blaine, James G. 154
Blow, Taylor 34
Boston, MA 84-85
Braille 89
Brain death 179-181
Brandeis (University) 84
Brandeis, Justice 110
Brennan, Justice 84-85, 116, 139
Burton, Justice 76
California 51, 59, 134, 165, 173
Capital punishment 119, 124, 126, 128, 130, 132
Cardozo, Judge 63, 162
Catholic Church 182-183
Casey, Bishop Lawrence B. 182
Censorship 89-92, 94
Civilian Exclusion Order 50-51, 53, 55-58
Civil commitment 170
Civilian Restrictive Order 56
Civil Rights Commission 101
Civil War 36
Clark, Justice Thomas 68-69

Clark, Attorney General Ramsey 124
Cleland, John 84-85
"Clear and convincing" standard 159, 161-162, 165, 169-174
Concentration camps 58
Common law 121, 137, 139, 161-163, 166, 172
Confession 96-98, 101, 106, 108, 112
Congress 26, 28-31, 33, 42-43, 45, 51-54, 56, 58, 60, 69, 73-75, 77, 101, 120, 130
Connecticut 24
"Cruel and unusual punishment" 116-123, 126-131, 177, 184
Curfew 50, 52-54, 63
Curtin, Thomas R., Esq. 191
Declaration of Independence 18-21, 23, 31
Defamation 146-147, 151, 153
Delmonico's 154
Deportation 62, 64, 170
Denaturalization 170
Detention center, military 50, 56, 57, 59, 64-65
DeWitt, General 60-61, 65
Discrimination 53, 58, 63-64, 119, 123, 126-127
Douglas, William O. 88, 116-117
Due Process 39-40, 62, 117-118, 129-130, 135, 137, 139-140, 167, 169-170, 174
Emerson, John 14
Eighth Amendment 116-120, 125-126, 128, 176, 184
Electrocution 128-129
England 20, 76, 119
Equal Protection Clause 127
Emotional distress, intentional infliction of 146-152, 156
Espionage 50, 52-53
Establishment Clause 68-69, 74-80
Ethics Committee 190
Evacuation 56-57, 65

Evidence 96, 98, 100-101, 105, 110, 112
Exclusion Order, see Civilian Exclusion Order
Executive Order 50-52, 60
Executive Branch 32, 53, 123, 137
Fifteenth Amendment 36, 39, 42, 45
Field, Justice 122
Fifth Amendment 97, 110-111, 137
"Fighting" words 155
First Amendment 68-69, 74-78, 80-82, 84-86, 89, 91-92,
  94, 138, 147, 149-150, 152-153, 155-156, 162, 176
Flag salute 70-71
Fortas, Justice 84
Fourteenth Amendment 36-39, 42-46, 68-69, 75, 84, 86,
  91, 116-118, 127-129, 134-135, 137-138, 141, 147,
  167, 176
Fourth Amendment 167
Frankfurter, Justice 76, 150
Freedom of the press 90, 92
Freedom of religion 75-77, 81, 177, 184
Freedom of speech 90-92, 150
Free Exercise Clause 69, 74-75, 77, 79
Free inhabitant 26-27
Georgia 116-117, 134-135, 139-140, 142-144
Georgia Central State Hospital 116, 125
Harper's Weekly 153
Harvard (University) 84
Harvard Medical School 180
Heterosexuals 139-140, 142, 144
Homosexuality 133, 137-140, 142-143
House Committee on the Judiciary 122
Holmes, Justice 150
Homicide 121, 169, 189
Hunt, Circuit Justice Ward 43, 48
Hughes, Chief Justice 177
"Ignorance of the law" 46

Illinois 14, 32-33
Insanity 116, 125
Informed consent 161-163, 166
Interrogation 96-98, 100-113
Incompetence 161, 163-166, 168-172, 177, 184, 186
Jackson, Justice Robert 59, 75, 76, 77, 81
Japan 50-55, 58-59
Japanese American Citizens League 65
Japanese Americans 49-56, 58, 62-63
Jasper County, MO 159
Jefferson, Thomas 74
Kidnapping 96, 112
Kings County, NY 102
Libel 91, 146-149, 151, 156
Lawes, Warden Lewis E. 124
Leopold and Loeb 124
Liberty interest 142, 167-168
Library of Congress 89
Lincoln, Abraham 154
Living Will, Missouri Statute 161
"Limited objective" standard 164
Lord's Prayer 68, 70-72, 80
Loeb, see Leopold
Louisiana 32-33, 129
Madison, James 73-74, 80
Magna Carta 120
Malice, actual 148-149, 156
Marshall, Chief Justice 98
Marshall, Justice Thurgood 116, 139
Maryland 24
Massachusetts 24, 84-86, 88-90
MIT 84
Mayflower Compact 73
McDougall, Walt 154
McGee, Dr. 178

Military Area 50-52, 56, 58
Military, U.S. 50-54, 56, 58-65
Militia law 28
Missouri 14-15, 17, 32-34, 36-38, 158-160, 166, 168-174
Missouri State Department of Health 158
Muir, Judge 187-188
Missouri Compromise 14, 33
"Mutt and Jeff" 105
Moral Majority 146
Morris County, NJ 176-177
Morse, Dr. Robert J. 178-179, 181
Naturalization 28, 44
Nast, Thomas 153-154
Neutrality 74, 77, 79-82
New Hampshire 24
New Jersey 39, 162, 176-177
Newton Memorial Hospital 177-178
New York State 43-45, 78, 90, 165
New York Legislature 129
Nineteenth Amendment 41
Norman Conquest 119
Northwest Ordinance 120
Ninth Amendment 134-135
Obscenity 84-94, 138
Obscenity Test, see Social Importance
Offensive Speech 145, 150, 152, 155
"Outrageousness" 149, 152, 154-156
Patel, U.S. District Court Judge Marilyn Hall 65
Parental rights, termination of 170, 171
Pearl Harbor 50
Pennsylvania 68-70, 80
Philadelphia, PA 68, 70
Phoenix, AZ 96, 112
Police brutality 101-102
Political cartoons/satirists 153-154

Powell, Justice Lewis 127
President's Commission on Law Enforcement
  & Administration of Justice 123
Privacy, right to 136, 138, 141-142, 161, 163, 166, 177,
  184-189
Privacy, invasion of 146-148
Putnam's Sons, G.P. 85
Public figures 149-151, 153, 156
Rape 96, 112, 116, 124
Rehnquist, Justice 127, 146-147, 158-159
Reed, Justice 129
Reckless disregard 149, 151, 156
Religious Freedom Amendment 75
Relocation 50, 56-58
Resettlement 56
Rhode Island 24
Right of choice 186
Roberts, Justice 76
Rochester, NY 42
Roosevelt, Franklin 50, 154
Roosevelt, Teddy 154
Rutledge, Justice 76-77
Sabotage 50, 52-53
St. Louis, City of 34
St. Louis, County of 36-38
St. Clare's Hospital 177-178, 182
San Leandro, CA 50-51
Secularism, religion of 80
Search and seizure 167
Self-incrimination 96-98, 100-101, 109-110, 113
Sing Sing 124
Self-determination 162-164, 189
Social Importance 84, 86-90, 92-93
South Carolina 120

State interests 135, 143, 150, 152, 163, 167, 169-170, 185-186
States rights 46
Stewart, Justice 78, 116
Stevens, Justice John Paul 139
Surrogate 164-165, 168-170, 186
Suicide 169
"Substituted judgment" 161, 165, 172-174
Taft, Judge Alphonso 74
Taney, Chief Justice Roger B. 14-15
Texas 123
"Third Degree" 101, 108
Treason 59-60
Tuttle, Judge 121
Tweed, William M. "Boss" 153
Tweed Ring 153-154
Unitarian Church 68, 70
Virginia 14, 120, 148
Waite, Chief Justice Morrison 36-37
Waiver of rights 96, 100, 110, 112-113
War Powers 50, 52
Warren, Chief Justice 77, 84, 96-97
Washington, DC 29, 134, 137
Washington, George 154
Webster's (Dictionary) 153
White, Justice Byron 92, 116, 134-135
Wickersham Report 101
Williams, Roger 74
Wisconsin 14, 32

Coming Soon in the Landmark Decisions Series

LANDMARK SEXUAL RIGHTS DECISIONS

LANDMARK RELIGIOUS FREEDOM DECISIONS

LANDMARK CIVIL RIGHTS DECISIONS

LANDMARK FREEDOM OF SPEECH DECISIONS

LANDMARK CRIMINAL JUSTICE DECISIONS

LANDMARK DECISIONS OVERRULED

Also Available From Excellent Books

LANDMARK DECISIONS OF THE UNITED STATES SUPREME COURT

SCHOOL DESEGREGATION

OBSCENITY

SCHOOL PRAYER

FAIR TRIALS

SEXUAL PRIVACY

CENSORSHIP

ABORTION

AFFIRMATIVE ACTION

BOOK BANNING

FLAG BURNING

MAUREEN HARRISON & STEVE GILBERT
EDITORS

ORDER FORM

Please send _____ copy(ies) of LANDMARK DECISIONS and
_____ copy(ies) of LANDMARK DECISIONS II

OUR GUARANTEE: Any Excellent Book may be returned at
any time for any reason and a full refund will be made.

Name: _____

Address: _____

City: _____ **State:** _____ **Zip:** _____

Price: $14.95 for LANDMARK DECISIONS
$15.95 for LANDMARK DECISIONS II
Shipping and handling included

Sales Tax: California residents add 7.25%

Mail your check or money order to: Excellent Books,
Post Office Box 7121, Beverly Hills, California 90212-7121